What You Feel, You Can Heal!

What You Feel, You Can Heal

A Guide For Enriching Relationships

John Gray Ph.D.

HEART Publishing
Mill Valley, California

Library of Congress Catalog Card No. 84-82045

Heart Publishing Company
Suite A-130
20 Sunnyside Ave.
Mill Valley, CA 94941

Printed in the United States of America

ISBN 0-931269-00-8 (Paperback)

Designed by Robert Herstek

To those strong people who are willing to feel and open their hearts, creating a better world for us all.

Acknowledgements

With deepest gratitude I wish to thank:

Bonnie Gray, my wife and partner, for her loving and devoted support which inspires me to ever-increasing heights;

Barbara DeAngelis, whose loving presence and editorial expertise assisted me greatly in the writing of this book;

Tamira Langton, for her continuous love and belief in me and all that I've written on the following pages;

Linda Lawson, for her understanding and implementation of these techniques as Director of the HEART Counseling Center;

Merril Jacobs, for her loving support of my artistic ability and her insightful proofreading of this manuscript;

Helen Francell, for her sensitive editorial efforts;

Robert Herstek, for his dedication, commitment and amazing skill in assembling and publishing this book;

Bob Hoffman and *Connie Berens*, for their diligent and generous efforts in producing this book;

All the thousands of graduates of my seminars for practicing the HEART techniques and proving their practical validity and giving me the confidence to develop the HEART Model;

and especially to Virginia Gray, my mother — I love you.

J.G.

Foreword

We all need to love and be loved, yet fulfilling this primary need can be one of life's greatest challenges. Creating loving and lasting relationships is a necessity if we are to maintain psychological health. But finding and sustaining loving relationships takes more than just good intentions, it takes skill, practice and a commitment to growing.

To truly give and receive love we must learn to give without expectations and receive without demanding. This unconditional love is not just an ideal but something we can realize through practice. The secret to developing this skill is learning to love yourself. As you grow in self love, your ability to give and receive love will grow automatically.

Unconditional love is realized when our hearts are full and overflowing. It is easy to love unconditionally when we are feeling positive and loved by others. It becomes difficult when we are feeling negative and unloved. At such times, when it is difficult to receive love and support from outside we must turn inside and give to ourselves. Then when we are feeling good about ourselves, it is not only easier to give but it becomes easier to communicate and negotiate the fulfillment of our own needs and wants. We become like a magnet which attracts more support.

What You Feel, You Can Heal clearly shows how unresolved negative emotions from the past restrict our ability to love ourselves as well as others. Through learning to feel and express our hidden feelings we can begin to love and accept parts of us that were lost in the past. We need not be prisoners of our past but can set ourselves free to share the richness of who we truly are and receive the support and recognition that we deserve. This book inspires us to be kinder to ourselves and to create loving and lasting relationships.

In this simple and useful book, you will learn practical techniques to enrich your relationships with greater love, communication and cooperation. Most of all, however, you will learn to love yourself which is the greatest love of all.

Harold H. Bloomfield, M.D.
Author of *Lifemates*

Table Of Contents

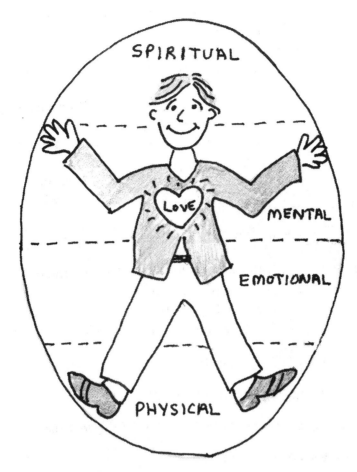

Without Love, all else will fail.

Chapter 1

Love: The Central Need

As human beings, we are incredibly complex with an endless stream of physical, emotional, mental and spiritual needs that must be satisfied. Frustration at any of these levels can produce suffering to the whole being. There is one need so fundamental and essential that, when not met, causes everything else to fail or fall short of fulfillment. That need is the need for love — love of others and love of yourself.

The major cause of human dissatisfaction and frustration is the absence of love. This fundamental human need outweighs all others. Without love you can never feel a genuine sense of fulfillment. It is the foundation of security upon which you can build a successful life. No matter what you possess, you cannot fully enjoy it unless you are loving yourself and sharing with people you care about. No matter how much you accomplish or acquire in life, it cannot supersede your basic need for love.

In essence, what I'm saying is that your biggest problem is your inability to satisfy your need for love and that because of it, you end up creating all sorts of other problems.

That need for love begins with your need to love yourself. When you are not able to love yourself, it becomes very difficult for others to love you. Self-love is essential if you are to receive the love you want and deserve.

The need for Love outweighs all of our other pursuits.

Every person has special qualities that make them unique.

Every one of us is born with a unique and special value. There is no one who can be a better you. You have a special place in this universe and a part of growing up is discovering your own niche — finding out what you have to offer, what you are here to do, and then doing it. This discovery will bring you deep fulfillment and enliven the core of your being. The only way to accomplish this task is to stop masking who you really are and to begin accepting and loving yourself the way you are.

You wouldn't be reading this book if you didn't love yourself. A part of you does love yourself enough to say: "I do deserve more love and I'm determined to get it. Maybe this book will help." At least you haven't given up on yourself.

Consider this line of questioning:

**Q: Why do you get upset when
people don't appreciate you?**
**A: Because you feel you deserve
to be appreciated.**

Q: Why do you dress in nice clothes?
A: Because you want people to like you.

Q: Why do you want people to love you?
A: Because you feel you deserve it.

Deep down inside, you want love, appreciation and acceptance from people because you feel you do deserve it. But you, like most people, have probably lost touch with that feeling of self-love that you had when you were a small child.

What Happens When You Love Yourself

When you love yourself in the presence of others, you are able to express your inner gifts and talents without fear or restriction. The more you love yourself, the more you are able to come out. The more you come out, the easier it is for people to appreciate the real you and not the image you project or the mask you wear. The more people appreciate and love you, the more you can love yourself. It is a cycle of increasing love and true self-expression.

I love myself more
I express myself more
People can love me more
I love myself more
etc.

When you don't love yourself and you mask your real self, the cycle works in the opposite direction of decreasing love and true self-expression.

I love my real self less
I express my real self less (I wear a mask)
People can love my real self less
I love my real self less
etc.

When you start loving yourself more, you are able to express more of your inner gifts and talents and allow others to love you more.

Loving yourself gives you the ability to love others.

The world is like a mirror showing us a reflection of who we are.

Loving yourself more gives you the ability to love and appreciate others more as well. The world becomes a different place. For each of us the world is like a big mirror, showing us a reflection of who we are. We each see the world through different-colored glasses, determined by the way we feel about ourselves.

People who hate the world hate themselves.

People who hate the world, hate themselves. Much of the time, when you are disapproving of others, it is really a part of yourself that you see and dislike. Learning to love yourself and to be yourself is the first step in learning to accept, value and love others, and enriching your relationships.

To start your journey towards loving yourself again, let's take a look at where it all began...

Where It All Began

You were born with an infinite supply of self-love. Self-love is a quality naturally instilled in every baby. Did you ever see a baby that didn't want love and attention, and make a big fuss when it didn't get its quota? Can you even imagine a baby complaining "Give me some space, you're smothering me with love"?

As little children, we all loved and accepted ourselves. Only now, as adults, we are afraid to show it or even admit it. We have learned that it can be very risky to love ourselves in the presence of other people and that it is much safer to hide our self-love.

I've found that there are five unconscious messages we receive while growing up that can keep us from fully loving ourselves for the rest of our lives. We were conditioned not to love ourselves in five basic ways. These messages are:

1. It's not O.K. to appreciate yourself
2. It's not O.K. to desire for yourself
3. It's not O.K. to be yourself
4. It's not O.K. to make mistakes
5. It's not O.K. to express yourself

**Loving yourself
can be very risky**

1. It's O.K. To Appreciate Yourself

Ever since you were young, you were taught that it is not OK to love and appreciate yourself. You learned that to appreciate yourself is vanity and vanity is not good. You learned that to show how much you really love yourself is dangerous - people will criticize you.

Imagine arriving at a party and someone walks up to you and says: "Gee, you look great." If you responded by agreeing with them: "I know, I look gorgeous tonight," they would probably walk away thinking you were really strange. In our society we learn that when you love yourself openly, others might accuse you of egotism and conceit, and they will reject you.

In an attempt to get love and support, you learn to hide your self-love and may even be in the habit of putting yourself down. Gradually, you begin to believe your own propaganda and your self-love gets repressed and forgotten.

You were probably taught that other people won't like you if you like yourself too much.

We learn very early to feel guilty about our desires.

2. It's O.K. To Desire For Yourself

While growing up, you learn very quickly that the world wasn't created for you alone and that you can't have whatever you want. You are made to feel selfish and bad for wanting more than you have. In an attempt to be good and lovable, you try to suppress your desires and as a result, you may become like a robot, acting out the desires of others in order to win their acceptance and love. You may even begin to feel guilty about your dreams and wants, feeling they are "selfish."

3. It's O.K. To Be Yourself

Children often get the message that in order to get love, they have to "earn" it or pay for it. You conclude that your worthiness is not in yourself, but in something else — your appearance, your actions, your success, or your ability to do what is expected of you. If you experienced love being turned on and off to you as a child, you probably decided that your worth and goodness depends on your ability to please other people and do what makes them happy. Your self-esteem becomes something based on how much you please others by being "good".

While growing up, you probably learned that to get love you had to pay for it.

15

Because you are not perfect, you will feel unworthy of such approval and you will gradually learn to mistrust love.

4. It's O.K. To Make Mistakes

Every child quickly catches on to the reality of conditional love; when we are right, we win and when we are wrong and make mistakes, we lose love.

At the other extreme is the child whose parents attempted to bestow him with unconditional love. Perhaps when you misbehaved or performed poorly or felt badly, your parents ignored the problem or mistakes, pretending everything was fine. As a result, you unconsciously sensed their disapproval or resentment but you never had an opportunity to be forgiven. In both cases, you know you are not perfect and you feel unworthy of approval when it is given. You learn to mistrust approval from others and fear their disapproval as well.

5. It's O.K. To Express Yourself

The result of your need to please your parents and peers in order to get their love is that you lose your spontaneous self-expression. You become preoccupied with becoming like other people and miss the opportunity to explore and express your own uniqueness.

When you suppress your inner potential, you live with a sense of inner frustration and failure because you have buried your potential for success. One part of you wants to express itself, but another part wants love and acceptance and will sacrifice self-expression in order to get it.

Some people are afraid to succeed and so they bury their potential.

If you cannot love yourself, then you lose your ability to truly receive love from others.

Learning To Trust Love

All of this conditioning to not be "yourself" in order to get love has an unfortunate result: you lose your ability to truly receive love from others. If a part of you is hiding who you really are, not expressing yourself fully or trying to be like others, you cannot trust the love and appreciation you get from the people you are trying so hard to please. When others express their love for you, a little voice inside says: "Yeah, sure, they wouldn't say that if they really knew me." You try hard to please others, knowing all along that the "real you" isn't coming out, and this prevents you from feeling good about whatever approval you do receive.

In the following chapter, we will explore the various ways you may be hiding yourself.

Chapter 2

How Are You Hiding Yourself?

The result of your attempt to feel loved and to please others is that, like most people, you have learned and adopted various behavioral strategies designed to get the approval and love you need. These strategies become like roles you play, or personality types you act out, whether consciously or unconsciously.

This chapter contains a list of some of the more common examples of personality types you may be acting out. You might notice a part of yourself described in several or even all of them. For each category, I also suggest a few hints for breaking out of these roles and starting to express the real you that is buried inside. These hints are far from complete. Later in this book, I'll offer you powerful and practical techniques for loving yourself and others more.

1. The Performer

This person was given a lot of love for performing and excelling as a child. Performance is the assumed condition for love and recognition. He is always trying to measure up to the expectations of others and many times self-imposes even higher expectations. He always feels pressured and driven to achieve and there is no time for rest. He cannot tolerate weakness or stupidity in himself or others and tends also to be very critical.

The Performer feels pressured to measure up. For him there is no rest; he feels driven to achieve and perform.

The Performer needs to relax more and discover that he can be loved even when he is not performing.

Secretly, the Performer feels he can never be good enough, since there is always room for more growth. This type may become very attached to people and positions, since a secret fear of rejection or abandonment motivates his behavior. He generally feels responsible for everything.

The Performer needs to relax more and discover that he can be loved even when he is not performing. Take more vacations and read romantic novels. Give yourself a break — the high blood pressure isn't worth it.

2. The Critic

The Critic is preoccupied with finding, pointing out and talking about the faults of others. He rejoices in criticizing and belittling those around him. He may hate part of himself, projecting that quality onto others and then becoming extremely critical and judgmental of them. Whenever he is afraid of being judged, he is quick to retaliate with a string of judgements, often sarcastic in nature. For him, the best defense is a strong and critical offense.

The Critic is obsessed with changing or even punishing others in a subconscious attempt to change himself. He is able to soothe his own feelings of inadequacy by proving the shortcomings of others.

If you have these traits, try to begin seeing yourself in all those that you judge and criticize. Imagine yourself in their footsteps — look for a way in which you are like them. Then forgive yourself and forgive them for not being perfect. Just as you are good at finding reasons to separate, try finding reasons to feel connected to others.

What the Critic hates about himself, he will find and criticize in others.

3. The Boaster

This person compensates for low self-esteem by always exaggerating the truth and bragging. While growing up, he learned that to get attention he had to dramatize and enlarge the truth. The Boaster doesn't plan to lie — it happens automatically. Even if the real truth is worthy of attention, he must enlarge it.

The Boaster has learned to get attention by dramatizing and exaggerating the truth.

Deep inside, the Boaster feels he is not good enough to warrant love and attention. He feels the truth is never enough for him to achieve the recognition he needs in his own eyes and in the eyes of others, so he stretches the truth.

The Boaster can never trust the love of others, for deep inside he knows he is lying. The closer people get, the more secretive and defensive he becomes. And the more he boasts, the less he trusts the attention and appreciation he gets.

The Boaster must practice being accurate in what he says and learn that others will still love him.

The Boaster needs to practice being very accurate in what he says. He should find someone who truly does care for him and share with that person all the lies and pretenses he can remember and see that he can be loved for who he really is. The Boaster must learn to trust again, both himself and others. He needs consistent and honest feedback. To be easy on him is not doing him any service.

Whenever something bad happens to a Victim, you can be sure their story gets a lot of mileage.

4. The Victim

This person was generally hurt very deeply at a young age and got a lot of sympathy. The Victim feels unworthy of love and support unless it is preceded by a great mishap or tragedy, or at least the telling of some past tragedy. Whenever something bad happens to the Victim, you can bet that story gets a lot of mileage. If you are getting a lot of love, attention and sympathy by telling your Victim stories, watch out — you are reinforcing a pattern of getting love through experiencing and communicating about pain and suffering. So if your stories get old and you want some love, presto! You will create a new dramatic tragedy. You might even use getting sick as a way of getting more love.

The Victim usually feels powerless in life and tries to control people by making them feel guilty. He refuses to take responsibility for his life, so, quite subconsciously, others get sucked into trying to please the Victim and make him happy. The Victim must learn to develop his own personal power through taking responsibility for his life. He must resolve his stored-up, repressed anger and practice forgiving others.

Victims must learn to develop their power by taking responsibility, expressing their anger and then forgiveness.

The Nice person is always doing what he "should" be doing and has lost touch with what he really wants.

5. The Nice Person

This person is always good-tempered, cheerful and very agreeable. He makes a great friend and generally has a lot of friends and acquaintances. The Nice Person learned early in life that compliance brings a reward, a smile or an embrace. He submits to every rule and regulation with mechanical precision. He is always doing what he "should" be doing, intent on pleasing others, saying "yes" to everyone. The Nice Person never gets angry, but learns to accept and adapt to every situation. He never rocks the boat.

On the surface, the Nice Person is happy and content to be a part of the group, but inside he is empty and alone. He is very afraid of being himself, for to do what he wants means risking disapproval. So, he has lost touch with what he really wants and who he really is. He has done everything right and according to the rules, but secretly feels controlled and cheated, lifeless and bored.

The Nice Person is trapped — he can never really open up because others would find out he is really not so nice. By being nice, he has successfully repressed his own special uniqueness and has become a non-person.

The Nice Person needs to practice saying "no" and meaning it. He needs to learn to express his anger. He must risk showing the not-so-nice person inside and see that not only will others still love him but that they may even feel closer to him because now he is more real.

The Nice person needs to practice saying "no," and meaning it.

The Self-righteous person can never admit that he is wrong,
for to confess his faults could mean the loss of love.

6. The Self-Righteous Person

This person has learned that if he is wrong, people will not love him
and will consider him bad. In order to get love, he attempts to be right at
all costs. He can never admit that he is wrong, for to confess his faults
and failures would mean the loss of love and would be very painful to
him. The Self-Righteous Person often tries to make others wrong in

order to be right himself. He has a rational excuse for everything he does. He could even become a great teacher. But don't try to have an argument with the Self-Righteous Person because it will sound more like he is lecturing you on why you are wrong and he is right.

The Self-Righteous Person needs to start practice saying: "I'm sorry," whenever he makes a mistake, even when he has a great excuse. Rationalization and justification are favorite ways of avoiding feelings, especially the feeling of guilt. This person needs to learn that others will love him, even if he is wrong or makes a mistake.

The Self-righteous person should practice saying: "I'm sorry," whenever he makes a mistake.

The Angry person feels ripped off by life and is constantly trying to get even.

7. The Angry Person

This person walks around with a chip on his shoulder. For him, anger is a protection; it is a roar to scare away adversity. The Angry Person feels an inner inadequacy and is always trying to protect himself. To compensate for that feeling of inadequacy, he refuses to be adequately satisfied by the outer world. Nothing can please him. He projects his own inadequacy everywhere, hence feeling frustrated and bitter towards the world.

The Angry Person feels ripped off by life and is constantly trying to get even. He gets angry at the drop of a hat and remembers every injustice he has ever experienced. He delights in the shortcomings and failings of others and thus becomes overly competitive.

The Angry Person is stuck in feelings of anger and blame as a cover-up for his own feelings of inadequacy and hurt. He must learn that he still deserves love even if he is inadequate in certain areas. Each day he should practice the Love Letter technique (taught later in this book) and forgiveness. Through loving and forgiving others, he will learn to truly love and forgive himself.

8. The Fake

This person has played so many roles that he doesn't know who he is anymore. Behind every mask is another. He is always acting according to how others will receive him. The Fake will not risk controversy. He is an expert at impressing others in order to be liked. He plays the roles he thinks others want him to play and in the process becomes a hypocrite and a fraud.

The Fake probably never felt appreciated for being himself while growing up, so he decided that in order to get love, he had to be someone else, whomever others wanted him to be. Unfortunately, he can never trust anyone's love or appreciation, because deep inside he knows he is a fake and that others don't know who he really is.

The Fake has played so many roles that often he loses sight of who he really is; behind every mask is another.

The Believer has become so dependent on others for truth that he loses touch with reality.

9. The Believer

This person has become so dependent on others for truth that he doesn't believe his own feelings. He learned growing up that to receive love, he merely has to agree and believe what others tell him. If you have a common belief, then the Believer is your friend, and if you contradict his belief, you are his enemy. The Believer loves to give away his own power and responsibility to others who can solve his problems for him. He expects you to love him because he agrees with you. If you disappoint the Believer's unrealistic expectations, he will withdraw his love and support.

The Believer has never gotten over the fact that his parents were not perfect. He always has high hopes, but is inevitably let down by others, and will continue to be until he starts to believe in himself.

The Believer must learn to take responsibility for his own life and forgive all the people who have let him down. He should question all he believes, and relate it to his own personal experience. The Believer needs to learn to trust his own feelings, instincts and choices and look to himself as the source of power and wisdom in his life.

The Believer needs to question all that he believes and relate it to his own personal experience.

The Shy person's basic reaction to people is fear. He has little confidence that he will be loved.

10. The Shy Person

This person's basic reaction to other people is fear. He fears their criticism, he fears their evaluation of him as a failure and he fears their inevitable rejection in the end. The Shy Person has little confidence that he is lovable to others. He has been taught that people will only accept him under certain conditions and if those conditions aren't present, he fears rejection. He may be an incredible musician or performer on stage, but offstage he becomes shy and insecure.

The Shy Person must learn to take risks. He should practice visualizing a risk and then act it out, gradually building up more confidence in himself and dispelling his fear of others. He needs to come out more and learn to trust himself and others again.

The Shy person should visualize a risk and then act it out and gradually build up more confidence.

The Show-off believes that what he owns will make up for what he fails to be himself.

11. The Show-Off

The Show-Off believes what he does or possesses will make up for what he fails to be himself. He seeks to compensate for his own lack of self-esteem by owning big things, hoping this will attract the attention and recognition he desperately needs. To the Show-Off, money is the symbol of love, and without it, he fears he will lose love. He cannot ask for love, but tries to buy it. He is unable to share his feelings directly, but does so by giving or withholding presents and material possessions.

Unfortunately, the Show-Off never feels worthy of the love he does receive, because he knows he is being loved for his achievements and possessions and not for being himself. He often feels used and unappreciated.

The Show-Off needs to practice sharing his feelings and allowing others to see who he is inside. He needs to work on his inner self-image and relax his outer image. Then he will learn that he can be loved for who he is and not for what he has or what he does.

The Show-off needs to practice sharing his feelings and allowing others to see who he is inside.

12. The Loner

This person is always proving that he doesn't need others. At some point while growing up, he didn't get the love and recognition he wanted, so he decided he didn't need it. The Loner has learned to become self-sufficient. Inside, he is an incredibly sensitive and caring spirit who has been hurt too many times. He has learned to "care less", to be detached from his feelings, for to feel them would be too painful.

The Loner feels guilty for needing so much love and thus he denies his needs. "I can do it alone," he proudly proclaims. "I don't need you." Because he doesn't express his needs clearly, he is continually disappointed and hurt in relationships. He will also resent feeling obligated to satisfy his partner's needs, just as he resents having his own needs. To the Loner, needs are a sign of weakness.

At some point, the Loner could not get the recognition and love he wanted and so decided he didn't need it.

***The Loner needs to share his needs and wants. He must
reveal to others his secret expectations and
disappointments.***

The easiest choice for the Loner is to just avoid relationships and
live alone. The more he feels his needs, the more he will separate and
retreat, thus pushing out the very love he needs so desperately.

The Loner must learn to share his needs and to show his hurt and
tears. He should reveal to others all of his secret expectations and
disappointments. Whenever he starts to sulk and retreat, he should find
someone he cares about and share his feelings. The Loner needs to learn
that need is not a dirty word and to find people in life who can fulfill his
needs for love and appreciation.

The Sacrificer has learned that to love means to sacrifice or to give up for another.

13. The Sacrificer

This person learned that to love means to sacrifice or to give up for another. Probably while growing up, the Sacrificer's parents never let him forget how much they sacrificed and how they expected the same from him. For him, loving is a tiresome matter because to show his love, he must always do what he prefers not to do, or give up what he wants to keep.

The Sacrificer can never be what he wants to be, for that would be too selfish. For him, selfless giving is not giving with no strings attached, but it is a giving up or self-denial with a definite expectation of receiving the same in return. The Sacrificer expects the recipient of his love to return his gift of love through an equally painful sacrifice. "I suffered for you, so you suffer for me." For him, suffering is a virtue and is symbolic of true love.

The Sacrificer must learn to lighten up the heavy load he has placed on love and relationships. He needs to heal built-up repressed anger and resentment towards his parents and others and to forgive them for laying a "heavy guilt trip" on him. The Sacrificer needs to learn to give love freely without expecting equal sacrifice in return, and at the same time, he must remember not to give up his own needs and desires all the time.

The Sacrificer needs to lighten up the heavy load he has placed on love and relationships.

How Successful Are You At Hiding Yourself?

Let's see how well you score. Give yourself points on a scale from 1 to 5 for each of the personality types - a '1' means you play that role rarely, a '3' means often, and a '5' means you fit the description perfectly. To familiarize yourself with these types even further, imagine your family and friends and see how they score. The more you can see these personality types in others, the better you can see them and change them in yourself.

	You	Mom	Dad
1. The Performer			
2. The Critic			
3. The Boaster			
4. The Victim			
5. The Nice Person			
6. The Self-Righteous Person			
7. The Angry Person			
8. The Fake			
9. The Believer			
10. The Shy Person			
11. The Show-Off			
12. The Loner			
13. The Sacrificer			

Well, how did you do? How did your family do?

Remember: **Until you are aware of what you are doing, you have no choice but to continue doing it.**

Practice the instructions for each of the personality types along with the HEART techniques taught later in this book (Chapter 8), and you will be well on your way to loving yourself more.

Having explored some of the reasons we don't fully love ourselves, let's now look at some of the reasons why our relationships don't fully manifest the love that they deserve. In Chapter 3, we will take a look at what happens in our relationships.

Chapter 3

What Happens In Relationships

It's easy to fall in love. But it's a lot harder to stay in love. We all want love to last. We all want to live happily ever after. No one decides to get married and says to their partner: "Hey, honey, I've been thinking. Let's get married and have a wonderful two or three years together. Then, let's get tired of each other and get divorced — what do you say?" or "Darling, let's live together and have a great sex life for five years, then let's start fighting, feel resentful, have some extramarital affairs and then split up." No one falls in love and plans to fall out of love. But it happens, and when it happens, it hurts.

No one falls in love and plans to fall out of love. But it happens, and when it does, it hurts.

What Is The Norm?

Approximately one out of every two marriages in the United States ends in divorce. Out of the couples who do remain married, it's certain that a good number are no longer in love or happy together, despite the fact that they aren't officially divorced.

These statistics are not encouraging. Their real message to you is that if you plan to get married, you have a fifty-fifty chance of getting a divorce. (If you are reading this and are already married or just in a relationship with someone, the same unpleasant forecast applies to you.) You don't have to be a gambler to see that these are pretty terrible odds. You probably wouldn't invest your money in a business deal if you were told you had a fifty percent chance of losing it. Yet, like most people, you continue to get involved in relationships without thinking much about how to avoid joining the ranks of the fifty percent that don't make it.

There's no way to definately insure that any relationship will last, but you can at least learn to preserve the love that you had.

Let's take a closer look at the fifty percent of relationships that "succeed." Stop right now and ask yourself this question: "How many couples do I know whom I admire, whose relationship seems like one I would like to have for myself?" If you are like most people, you will have a hard time coming up with many examples of "good relationships." Between forty and seventy percent of married couples aren't satisfied with their partners and have had outside affairs. One recent survey showed that the greater the household income, the more affairs the couples had. It's obvious from these statistics that money is not the solution to marital happiness. The American Dream of a house, two cars and a happy family has ended in divorce all too many times.

When you're not satisfied with your present partner, you may begin to fantasize about others.

Some people keep up the appearance of a loving relationship when really the love has died.

Many people who stick it out in relationships aren't even able to look at their problems and admit to themselves and their partner that they aren't satisfied. They pretend to be happy when they are really feeling resentful, sad or numb. They must pretend because it would hurt too much to look at the truth. They are afraid to look at their problems because they don't have a solution. So they keep up the appearance of a relationship while all the time they are dying inside. Sometimes the loneliest place in the world is lying next to someone who doesn't love you anymore or someone you have stopped loving. How many times have you felt surprised when you heard friends of yours were getting a divorce or splitting up? On the surface everything looked great, but the love was dead.

What Are The Options?

Most people don't know how to solve their problems with love and relationships, and end up approaching those problems in one of several ways.

The first option, of course, is to just ignore the problems and hope that they will go away. Another method is to justify the problem and tell yourself that there is no such thing as the "perfect" relationship, and to expect more is immature and unrealistic. You can also try blaming it all on your partner. You may even leave that partner and find another, only to find yourself facing the same problems all over again. Some people go from partner to partner, trying to avoid conflict and problems. And others decide that it is less scary to stay stuck in a relationship than to risk leaving it, and they just give up. If you are one of these people who has just given up, I hope that reading this book will give you the courage to look at your problems and begin solving them, rather than accepting a life devoid of love.

One of the ways we deal with our problems is to blame them on other people.

Contrary to popular belief, relationships do not have to be doomed to mediocrity and boredom.

Have you ever felt: "I love my partner, but I'm no longer *in* love?" Unfortunately, the typical response to this complaint by family, friends and even many psychologists is: "Don't be immature. Face the facts — romantic love can't last. It's a tradeoff; you sacrifice passion for security." Contrary to popular belief, love and romance **can** last. Relationships do not have to be doomed to mediocrity and boredom. That flame of love and excitement that you shared in the beginning can remain burning and can even burn brighter.

Think back to a time when you saw a couple really enjoying each other's presence, looking very much in love. You probably assumed that they had just met or that they were having an affair. This negative conditioning about love lasting is very deeply ingrained in us from an early age.

Some people are outraged when they see two people in love.

Who Taught You How To Love?

You may not enjoy reading this next line, but *you learned how to love and have relationships by watching your parents when you grew up.* Most of this "education" occurred before the age of six, and you may be very unconscious of its influence on you. If you saw your parents lying to one another, you learned to lie. If you saw them hiding their true feelings, you learned to hide yours. If you saw them punish each other, you learned to punish and withhold your love. Long before you had your first real intimate relationship, you were thoroughly trained and conditioned, and unfortunately most of that conditioning taught you more about how not to love and communicate than about how to love and effectively communicate your feelings.

**Would you like to have a relationship
just like your parent's relationship?**

Long before you had your first intimate relationship, you were thoroughly trained and conditioned.

In order to start making love work admit to yourself that you need to learn more about it.

Relearning Love

If you want a relationship that is better than the one your parents had, if you want love to work for you, you have to work at it. Start by admitting to yourself that you need to learn how to make love work and that from looking around at everyone you know, you are not alone. Let go of your pride and feel the need you have deep inside for more intimacy, appreciation and love. The easiest way to learn is to pretend that you don't know anything about love. Try adopting beginner's awareness as you take this next step.

Enriching your relationships is an art and a science, just like building a bridge, making a meal, or playing an instrument. It takes skill and practice and daily application of those skills. Like all arts and sciences, enriching your relationship will seem like a mystery, like something impossible to comprehend until you have worked with it long enough to master it. Then it will be second nature.

Enriching your relationship can be learned. Already in the my seminars I have taught thousands of people to do so. Read on with an open mind and a willingness to practice mastering love .

Enriching Relationships

Everyone is always trying to enrich their relationships either consciously or unconsciously. No matter how much someone may act like they don't care, you can bet that underneath their defensive armor is a gentle spirit that wants to love and be loved. Behind every motive and action is the desire to be loved and appreciated and a longing to share ourselves with others.

Behind every scary front is a gentle spirit that wants to love and be loved.

***People are frustrated trying to make relationships work
because they have not learned a successful method.***

If everyone is trying to be more loving and kind to one another,
why are so many marriages breaking up and families being torn apart?
Why are there so many lonely people in the world? Why do people
continue to hurt one another?

Talking about love and having good intentions are just not enough.
After many years of counseling couples who had problems in their
relationship, I came to realize that in most cases there was really nothing
wrong with the people who came to me for counseling. However, there
was something wrong with the methods they were using in trying to
enrich their relationships. Most people start out attempting to work on

their relationships and end up frustrated and hopeless. In many cases, because they have not learned effective communication skills, the more they try to 'fix' their relationship, the worse it gets. As a result, the problems get ignored and accumulate over time. People unnecesarily accept the state of their relationships because they have no workable solution; they have no choice but to accept or try again with somebody new.

The more you try to change who you are in order to please others, the less you are able to love who you really are.

As a result of unsatisfactory relationships, many people today are obsessed with changing themselves, hoping that when they change, their life will improve. Creating more love in your life has nothing to do with changing who you are or with trying to change others. As a matter of fact, that just gets in the way. The more you try to modify your behavior in order to act like you think you "should" act, the less you will be yourself and the harder it will be for you and others to love you.

There is nothing wrong with change except when it prevents you from being who you really are. As long as change is motivated by self-hatred, it can never create more love. You may become more powerful; you may get a better job; you may even make new friends. But you're not going to love yourself more. You may succeed at convincing others that you are more worthy of their love, but deep down inside you will never feel truly loved and accepted for just being you.

As long as self-improvement is motivated by self-hate, it can never create more love.

Many times you may tell the truth but leave out the important parts. Telling the complete truth is more than being honest.

Chapter 4

The Essential Key:

Telling The Complete Truth

After eleven years of developing elaborate schemes for editing and modifying behavior with varying degrees of success, I discovered the essential key for learning to love yourself and enrich your relationships.

You must be able to share and express the complete truth about yourself and your feelings.

Telling the complete truth is different from being honest or not lying. Many times you tell the truth but leave out the important parts. Or, if you don't like the truth, you create a new truth.

Do you ever smile when you are really angry?

Have you ever acted mean and angry when deep inside you were really afraid?

Do you ever laugh and make light of something when you feel very sad and rejected?

Have you ever blamed another when you were the one feeling guilty?

This is what I mean by not telling the complete truth.

Most people are masters of disguising what they really feel.

Communicating the complete truth about your feelings is essential. It is the first step in resolving emotional tension and enriching your relationships with others. Before you can communicate the truth about what you feel, you have to know what you are feeling in the first place.

As human beings, we are experts at hiding the truth about what we are feeling. We become masters of disguising what we really feel inside, and therefore we end up hiding and suppressing who we really are. You may become so good at hiding the truth from yourself that you even start to believe your own lies. Gradually you may lose touch with what you really feel, and even if you want to tell the truth about what is going on inside, you can't.

Your ability to feel love is directly proportional to your ability to tell the complete truth. The more turth you have in your life, the more love you will experience. Honest relationships with direct and effective communication are a source of increasing love and self-esteem. Many times we seek out relationships in order to protect ourselves from the truth. We have a sign up saying: "If you don't tell me the truth, then I won't tell you the truth". These relationships can be easy and comfortable but do no service to increasing your self-love and self-worth.

Your ability to feel love is directly proportional to your ability to tell the complete truth.

Our emotions are like an iceberg; we generally show only a small fraction and the rest remain submerged.

The Iceberg Effect

The first step in telling the complete truth in your life is knowing what it is. Most of us are unaware of the complete truth; this phenomenon is called the Iceberg Effect. If you came upon an iceberg floating in the Arctic Ocean, you would only see one-tenth of it — nine-tenths of the ice block remains submerged beneath the surface. Your emotions are similar to that iceberg. Most of the time, just a fraction of how you really feel shows to others and even to your conscious mind, while the majority of your emotions lie hidden deep inside of you. Thus, it becomes difficult to communicate the complete truth about your feelings because they remain a mystery even to you.

Living In Your Heart
And Not In Your Head

Repressing your feelings is actually a safety mechanism you've developed over the years. Unable to cope with and express the truth about your emotions, you learn to hide those feelings deep inside and hope that they just go away. Through years of rejecting and suppressing your feelings, you start to acquire the unfortunate and unhealthy habit of automatically repressing any unsafe, unacceptable or confusing emotions. You learn only to express those feelings that won't disturb or threaten your life or others, thereby insuring safety and acceptance. You become a stranger to your own feelings. You begin to figure out in your head what to feel, rather than simply and spontaneously feeling from your heart.

As a result of repression, you stop feeling and start figuring out how you should feel.

Recovering buried emotions is essential for feeling motivated and purposeful.

What Are You Really Feeling?

Locating buried emotions is absolutely essential to your growth because to the extent that you suppress and bury your feelings, you will lose contact with who you are and what you really want.

In my years of researching human emotions, I have discovered a universal map of feelings to help you understand the maze of your emotions. When you are upset or unable to emotionally cope with a given situation, you are subconsciously experiencing various levels of feelings at the same time.

The levels are:

1. **Anger,** Blame and Resentment
2. **Hurt,** Sadness and Disappointment
3. **Fear** and Insecurity
4. **Guilt,** Remorse and Regret
5. **Love,** Understanding, Forgiveness and Desire

The complete truth has many different levels. It is perfectly normal to have many conflicting emotions at the same time.

By fully expressing all your negative emotions, you can spontaneously experience your love and understanding.

The complete truth about how you are feeling has many levels. Normally you are only aware of one emotion at a time, but the rest are all there as well. If all of these levels can be fully experienced and expressed, the emotional upsets can be easily resolved. Each emotion must be fully experienced and expressed for the successful completion of the process — if not, the feelings around any upset will never be fully resolved and will most likely be repressed inside of you, creating more emotional baggage for you to carry around from relationship to relationship.

By fully expressing all of the negative emotions, you can spontaneously experience your love and understanding again.

Most communication problems stem from only communicating part of the truth, and not expressing the complete truth. Often when people tell the truth, they leave out many of the feelings they are having and focus on one of the above levels, excluding the others. Underneath all negative emotions are positive emotions — underneath all anger and hurt is a feeling of love and a willingness to connect and be close. The people who make you the most angry are the people you care about the most. When something someone does interferes with your ability to love that person, the first four levels of emotion will be activated. **The problem arises when you communicate the anger or hurt and neglect to express the complete truth about the love underneath.**

Underneath all negative emotions is love and the desire for connection. The only way to uncover that love is to experience and express all those other emotions piled up on top. Failure to feel and express all our feelings prevents us from tapping into the vast emotional resources of love and confidence within our hearts.

Underneath all negative emotions is love waiting to gush forth.

When you don't fully express all the levels of your feelings, you may get stuck on one level.

Getting Stuck

Have you ever felt stuck in being angry even when you didn't want to be angry anymore?

Have you ever felt stuck in feeling sad, hurt or depressed, and nothing seemed to get rid of that gloomy feeling?

Have you ever felt frozen with fear and no matter how hard you tried, you couldn't snap out of it?

These are a few examples of what happens when you don't accept and express all of the feelings inside of you. Your inability to recognize and express the full range of feeling will cause you to stay stuck at one level of emotion and prevent you from fully feeling your positive emotions.

Men have difficulty showing vulnerable feelings because they were not given support to cry or feel hurt.

While growing up, we are all taught in various direct or indirect ways NOT to express all of the feelings inside. Little boys are taught: "Big boys don't cry — be strong." The message is that they don't have permission to show their vulnerable feelings. They are given permission to be aggressive, because that's supposedly masculine. In many cases they are taught that they can show their anger but that it isn't safe for them to show hurt or fear, for other boys might make fun of them or beat them up.

You may become stuck feeling angry or frustrated if you are unable to feel and express your more vulnerable feelings.

As a result, when an adult male has a strong emotional reaction, he may tend to get stuck on the level of anger and blame since it isn't safe for him to express the other more vulnerable levels. Often men will stay stuck in their angry feelings until they get even or until they repress the feelings entirely and shut down, becoming unreachable. I have worked with innumerable men who, when given permission to express their hurt, fear and guilt, experienced a tremendous emotional and physical release, letting go of the anger and feeling the love again. **All family violence is the result of unresolved anger.**

Unfortunately, if a man feels threatened, the last thing he feels safe doing is admitting that he is vulnerable and feels hurt or fear. So he will probably just pretend he doesn't care, which causes him to stay stuck in feeling angry or frustrated. Staying angry is one of the more popular ways of resisting our hurt and sadness. The angriest people I know are the ones who have the most hurt inside. The louder they scream and yell, the longer and harder they would cry if only they'd give themselves a chance. If you get angry more than you would like to, you need to learn to cry again.

By expressing the hurt and guilt which hides behind your anger you can easily release the anger and allow love to flow again.

Women tend to get stuck in their vulnerable feelings because they were not given permission to express their angry feelings.

For most women, the situation is reversed. Little girls are generally taught never to express anger and hostility. It's not nice to get angry or scream — Daddy won't like it, and neither will other men.

Many women are taught that they *can* display vulnerability. They can cry all they want to, and are even programmed to feel afraid. So as an adult, when a woman has something painful happen to her, she will tend to cry and feel afraid but probably will not overtly express her anger. Crying or criticism becomes a cover-up for anger and rage. And because that rage can't come up and the woman is stuck in her sadness, she may eventually become hysterical. I've worked with countless women who felt stuck in grief and hurt. After teaching them how to express anger, I've watched them miraculously recover and feel alive, loving and less critical.

If you are not able to fully express your anger (in a non-destructive way, of course) you may be walking around afraid, hopeless or depressed most of the time. **Depression is not intense sadness — it is suppressed anger that has been redirected at yourself.** Depressed people usually feel tired and lifeless because they are using up their vital energy to keep that anger and rage from coming out. If you are very depressed, you need to work on healing your old relationships, first by expressing your anger for others, then your anger at yourself, working your way back through all the other emotional levels until you arrive at the love and forgiveness.

When you repress your negative emotions, you also repress your ability to love.

Chapter 5

What Happens When You Don't Tell The Truth

Not telling the truth in a relationship is like not watering a plant — you end up killing something that once was alive and growing. The inevitable result of holding back the truth from someone you care for is that you end up holding back the love as well. After some time in a relationship where the truth is not expressed, you will look back and wonder: "What happened to that juicy feeling? Where did the magic go?" The answer is that the love and magic are buried under piles of uncommunicated emotions. You simply cannot repress your negative feelings (anger, fear, hurt, guilt) and expect the positive emotions to remain lively. **When you numb yourself to your undesirable emotions, you are numbing your ability to feel positive emotions as well.**

The long-term effects of not telling the truth to yourself or others and of pushing down your feelings is that you lose your ability to feel positive emotions like joy, excitement and passion. The dictionary defines passion as "an intense feeling." Every time you suppress a feeling you don't want to deal with, you are systematically destroying your ability to feel, and step by step you are killing the passion in all of your relationships.

Repression gradually numbs both your negative and positive feelings.

The four R's are the vital signs to watch for if you want to keep love alive!

The Warning Signs - The "Four R's"

I've discovered that there are four warning signs in every relationship that signal when the emotional connection is weakening and you are proceeding rapidly towards the loss of love in that relationship. I call these the "four R's." The four R's are the inevitable consequences of not telling the complete truth.

If you want to avoid the loss of love and feeling in a relationship and if you want to keep the passion alive, be on the lookout for the four R's. When you notice any one of the four R's, it's time to start telling the complete truth about your feelings. The four R's are:

1. Resistance
2. Resentment
3. Rejection
4. Repression

The death of a relationship occurs in four stages.

The sign of resistance is when you start noticing things about your partner that you don't like.

1. Resistance

In any normal human relationship there will be certain levels of resistance between two people. **Resistance** occurs when you notice yourself starting to resist something another person is saying, doing, or feeling. You start criticizing them in your mind, and you may notice yourself pulling away a little bit. Example: I'm at a party with my partner and she starts to tell the same story she always tells at parties, a story I've heard many times before. This time I notice myself feeling **Resistance** to her, a feeling inside like: "Oh no, there she goes with that story again." Or, your husband reminds you to pay a bill, and you notice yourself turning off to him somewhat, just for a moment.

The way most people handle **Resistance** is to ignore it and pretend it's not there. You may have thoughts like: "Oh, it's no big deal," or Don't be so critical; after all, no one's perfect" or "Just forget it. Why rock the boat?"

If you don't tell the truth about your resistance and resolve it with your partner, those little resistances build up and turn into the second R, Resentment.

2. Resentment

Resentment is a much more active level of resistance. It is intense dislike and blame of the other person for what they are doing. The other person really starts to annoy you. You may find yourself getting angry over small things, blowing them out of proportion. If I hear my partner tell that story enough times without communicating my resistance, the day will come when I no longer simply resist hearing that story, I will really resent it. I may feel: "Oh I *hate* when she tells that story, she is making such a fool of herself."

Resentment is usually accompanied by an internal experience of anger and tension. You are separating from your partner emotionally. Anger, frustration, annoyance, sharpness and hate are all symptoms of stage two, **Resentment.**

If you don't tell the truth about your resentment and resolve it with your partner, it builds up and turns into the third R, Rejection.

Anger, frustration, hate, revenge, annoyance, sharpness and blame are all the symptoms of unexpressed resentment.

83

3. Rejection

Rejection occurs when so much resistance and resentment has built up that it becomes impossible for you to stay emotionally connected to the other person, and you pull away. You are turned off emotionally and sexually. You may just say: "I don't want to discuss this any more." You may leave the room, you might storm out of the house, or you might just shut down and refuse to acknowledge the other person or pay attention to them. The signs of **Rejection** are: not wanting to be with your partner; always polarizing with whatever point of view they take; fantasizing about other people or having affairs. **Rejection** is the natural consequence of carrying around stored-up resentment. You cannot be near or relate to your partner without feeling all of your accumulated tension and resentment, so you just push them away in order to get some relief.

During this third stage, your sex life will deteriorate tremendously if it hasn't already. You may find yourself feeling you still love your partner, but you are no longer attracted to them, you are no longer "in love." You may feel repelled or disgusted at the thought of sex, or simply feel you just have no interest in sex anymore.

If you believe in divorce, you will probably decide to split up in this third stage. If you end a relationship while it is in the **Rejection** stage, the breakup will be painful and bitter.

If you don't tell the truth about your feelings of Rejection and resolve them with your partner, your Rejection builds up and turns into the next level of separation, Repression.

Unexpressed resentment inevitably turns into rejection ; you stop wanting to be with your partner.

4. Repression

Repression is the most dangerous of the four R's. It occurs when you are so tired of resisting, resenting and rejecting that you successfully repress all of your negative emotions to "keep the peace," for the sake of the family, or to look good to the world. In this fourth stage, you feel: "It's just not worth fighting over anymore; let's forget the whole thing; I'm too tired to deal with this."

Repression is a state of emotional numbness. You numb yourself to your feelings in order to be comfortable. The numbness spills over into the rest of your life. You lose your enthusiasm and aliveness. Life may become predictable and boring — it isn't painful, but it isn't joyful either. You may feel physically tired much of the time.

The tricky thing about **Repression** is that from the outside looking in, a couple in this stage may appear to be happy. They probably are nice and polite to each other and rarely fight, and you may think they have a great relationship, until one day you hear that they are getting a divorce.

Even more dangerous is the couple that is so repressed that they think they don't have any problems. They have given up their youthful, romantic dreams, and have accepted the status quo. They have learned what to expect and what not to expect. They have convinced themselves that they are happy. This couple is in trouble because until they admit that they would like improvement in the relationship, the relationship will stay where it is.

After rejection, you automatically repress your frustration and make everything OK. You stop caring about things.

Every time you have an argument, you probably move through the four R's.

Some people are so good at repressing that it happens automatically in a split second and they are totally unaware.

The four R's not only describe the stages of loss of love in a relationship over a long period of time, but also the mechanics of repressing feelings. Every time you repress an emotion, you go through these four stages. By repressing your emotions enough times, your relationship moves through the different stages. Each time you have an argument, you go through the four R's. You can go through the four R's in a matter of days, hours, minutes or even seconds.

Some people are such experts at repressing their feelings that they move automatically from **Resistance** right down to **Repression** in a few moments without even realizing what they are doing. Remember, the four R's apply to all of your relationships — not just with a lover, but with your parents, your children, your boss, your friends, and even yourself.

The truth can release the abundance of love within your heart.

Every time you express the complete truth about your feelings and get back to the love inside, you are increasing your ability to love. Every time you suppress the complete truth and automatically repress your feelings, your ability to love decreases. From this new perspective, you can see what went wrong in the past. By learning and practicing the techniques in this book for expressing the complete truth, you can quickly recover your ability to feel and to love. If you are stuck in any of the four R's, you will be able to move right back into feeling "in love."

Sometimes when you tell the complete truth, it may not look like progress because as you heal repressed feelings, you may move backwards through the stages from **Repression,** to **Rejection,** to **Resentment,** up to **Resistance.** But when you're finished — you are free to feel clear and loving again. This principle is dramatically demonstrated in the treatment of autistic children. If you express love to a repressed autistic child by holding it, it will move sequentially back through the four R's. First it will not respond and then it will reject your love and try to run away. If you hold on, the child will become extremely resentful and struggle against you. Eventually, it will simply resist a little and then accept your embrace with enthusiastic appreciation. As you begin to love your partner more, they may at first not care and they may reject your loving attempts. You may then evoke their scorn or resentment. But if you persist, they will eventually respond with great love and appreciation.

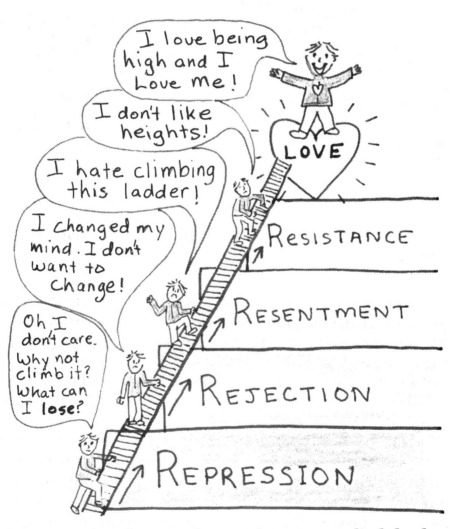

By expressing the complete truth, you can climb back through the four R's and feel alive and loving again.

The Reasons You Repress Your Feelings

Any feeling that threatens your ability to love or to be loved is a sure target for **Repression.** If you judge your emotions to be incompatible with your self-image, you will end up repressing them. You may also repress certain feelings which were never expressed by your parents while you were growing up. For instance, a child from a non-demonstrative family may have a tendency to repress emotions of tenderness and affection. A child who grew up in a family that never expressed anger may repress his feelings of anger.

The emotions you permit in your conscious awareness are the feelings you feel are "safe" to express. Your value judgements play a major part in repression — you will tend to label certain emotions "good" or "bad", "right" or "wrong," depending on your background and experience. For instance, you may feel it is "good" to feel grateful but "bad" to feel angry or jealous.

Any feeling that threatens our ability to be loved or to give love is a target for repression.

By burying your emotions, gradually you become numb to life and love.

Feelings Never Die

Most people try to "control" their feelings and the way they do this is usually to move through the four R's and resist, resent, reject and repress. Repressing your feelings does not eliminate them. Feelings never die. They refuse to be silenced. When you finally "forget" about a negative or unpleasant emotion, you may feel victorious, but the battle has just begun. It takes a tremendous amount of emotional and physical energy to hold down your feelings. Living becomes a struggle to stay in control.

Repressing your feelings will influence your personality, whether you like it or not, by secretly motivating much of your behavior. Repressing feelings may affect you undesirably in three basic ways:

1. You may numb your ability to feel positive emotions.
2. You may overreact to people or circumstances in the present.
3. Your body may express the tension from holding on to repressed emotions through physical symptoms and disease.

1. Becoming numb

Repressing your feelings gradually numbs your ability to feel. Your heart becomes cold and the well of love inside goes dry. Your childlike enthusiasm for living, loving and learning diminishes. Your creativity is

Repressed feelings do not die — they come back to haunt us.

Suppressed feelings build up until you either explode irrationally or you repress them by becoming numb to your feelings.

significantly reduced. You become a passionless witness to the process of living. The only answer is to take the chance to feel, and through working with all your feelings, to come alive again.

2. Are you overreacting?

Repressed feelings that you carry around may be responsible for you reacting inappropriately to people or circumstances in your life. Storing up unexpressed emotions can make you irrational, irritable, prone to temper tantrums or fits of depression at the drop of a hat. They can cause your attitudes to shift dramatically. Unresolved emotions from your past may confuse your emotions in present time. If I carry around a lot of suppressed guilt, I may become afraid of receiving punishment from all authority figures — policemen, bosses, the IRS — even if I'm not doing anything wrong or illegal. If I carry around a lot of repressed fear, I may unconsciously avoid meeting people or consciously tell myself I don't like them.

As adults, we are constantly living out repressed feelings from childhood. If you have a lot of repressed anger towards your domineering mother, for instance, you may interpret any suggestions or helpful advice from women as their attempt to control you. Unless you are aware of the process that is taking place, you will probably repress your feelings all over again and the cycle will continue.

Most people are unconscious of this phenomenon and you may think it does not apply to them. But think of all the times you have felt afraid or nervous when there was no apparent reason or the times you became irritable when there was no real cause, or the discomfort you feel in certain situations which are comfortable to others. For example: going up to a stranger and talking to them may be comfortable and easy for one person and hard for another. Or speaking in front of a group may be easy for one person and hard for another.

Repressed feelings cause us to react inappropriately to people and circumstances.

Repressed emotions can make you irritable, irrational, and prone to temper tantrums.

Unfortunately, in an attempt to further repress uncomfortable emotions, millions of people abuse their bodies with drugs, alcohol, cigarettes, overeating and overworking. These are popular and generally accepted means by which you can temporarily suppress unpleasant emotions. You are not only damaging your body by subjecting it to these experiences, you are damaging your ability to function as a feeling, emotionally healthy person as well.

When old repressed feelings suddenly come up in a new relationship you may feel your partner has changed overnight.

99

Repressed fears may motivate us to avoid meeting people that could love us.

More and more doctors today are realizing the importance emotions play on our physical health. Crying has been discovered to be an important physical discharge of harmful chemicals and simultaneously releases the emotional tension which is vital to prevent dis-ease in the body. For children as well as adults, crying in the right measure should be encouraged.

3. Are you beating up your body?

Your mind and body are intimately connected. Each is there to serve the other. If you choose to repress an uncomfortable emotion, your body may try to "help" resolve the tension you've created by releasing that tension for you through various physical symptoms.

Repressed feelings may become expressed through physical symptoms.

One of the more popular ways of avoiding feelings is overeating.

Physical symptoms are often related to the emotional dis-ease you are feeling:

Muscular tension — "He's a pain in the neck."

Headache — "I don't want to think about it anymore."

Viruses and colds — "I've decided to act cold to her."

Arthritis — "I was scared stiff" or "I guess I'm just set in my ways."

High Blood Pressure — "He really blew his top" or "I'm under so much pressure."

Respiratory — "I feel like this job is suffocating me."

Constipation — "I can't seem to let go of the past."

Heart Disease — "She broke my heart"

Fever — "Boy, he has a hot temper."

Recent psychological and medical research has revealed that certain personality types are more prone to cancer and heart disease than others. In one survey, the majority of cancer patients questioned admitted that they hadn't expressed strong emotions such as crying or angry outbursts with any consistency for years at a time, and they prided themselves on their ability to control their feelings. More and more, physicians are realizing the value of emotional release and expression in total physical well-being. Although a great deal of physical distress has its origin in repressed emotional distress, once it reaches the physical level, the body, mind and spirit must all be healed together.

Crying in the right measure should be encouraged.

Love initiates the release of repressed feelings.

Chapter 6

Feelings Are Your Friends

The ability to feel emotion is a gift we all share as human beings. Often, however, you may not like what you are feeling. Every emotion has a purpose and that emotion will remain with you until that purpose is realized and understood. Your feelings are like messengers from your subconscious to your conscious mind. Until you receive the message, the messenger will stand patiently at your door.

What are the messages your feelings bring to you?

Anger arises to tell you that what is happening to you is undesirable.

Hurt or Sadness arises to tell you that you have lost or are missing something you want or need.

Fear arises to warn you of the possibility of failure, loss or pain.

Guilt arises to remind you that in some way you are responsible for causing an undesirable result or circumstance.

The way to understand your emotions and what they are telling you about your life is to express them. **You cannot understand what remains unexpressed.**

Have you ever noticed that just by talking about a problem with a friend, you realize the solution? Through expressing the complete truth about all of your feelings, you can eventually realize the loving intention underneath all of your negative emotions.

Your feelings are like messengers. Until you receive their message they wait at your door.

Healing Repressed Feelings

An intimate relationship is the ideal setting for healing repressed feelings. When you find someone you feel safe with and loved by, all your repressed feelings begin to surface in an attempt to be healed. Through honest and loving personal relationships, you can not only learn to master the everyday tension which arises between you and another person, but you can use the relationship as an opportunity to heal old hurts, thus enabling you to become a more powerfully loving and lovable person.

Healing your feelings is an ongoing process. Whenever you get to a new level of love and closeness in your relationships, a new level of deeply repressed feelings will surface in order to be healed. The degree of intimacy determines the intensity of release. Without an understanding of the four R's and the five different levels of emotions, you might think you are going crazy; the more you love your partner, the more tension may seem to arise between you. But with dedication and commitment to growth, you will soon learn how much easier it is to tell the complete truth about your feelings and resolve the tension, rather than hiding the truth from yourself and those you love.

When you are living alone in your own separate world, it is very easy to continue repressing your feelings. This is why some people avoid relationships. It would take them too much effort and energy to continue repressing their feelings around another person. These people can only stand relationships for a certain amount of time and then they leave, either physically or emotionally, by shutting down their feelings altogether. You know you are resisting dealing with some repressed feelings when you leave your partner and feel relief.

It's very easy to hide from your feelings when you live in your head and avoid relationships.

This is why so many people cry for space in relationships. They walk around with all of these repressed emotions, and are pretty successful at holding them down until they come home at the end of the day and see each other. As soon as they start to open up, all of the unexpressed feelings of the day begin to surface. Rather than deal with them, it is simpler to just stay shut down. The last thing I may want to think about after work is what a hard day I had, but if I don't let those feelings out in the presence of my wife and release all the anger, hurt and fear, I will end up repressing them, and repress a part of my love for her as well.

This is not to undermine the need to be alone at times. We all need time alone and time away from any relationship to stay in touch with who we are. The need for autonomy is equally important as the need to share but should not be used as an excuse to deny one's feelings.

It is very difficult to repress your feelings all day and then come home and be loving!

Bringing up past repressed feelings is useless without also learning to resolve the emotional problems of the present.

Healing The Past With Therapy

Many people choose to work on healing their repressed emotions through counseling or therapy. A lot of therapies attempt to deal only with old repressed traumas, and neglect teaching a person how to resolve the emotional problems of the present. You cannot resolve past traumas without also learning to resolve your emotions in present time. If you decide to work with a therapist, make sure he or she can guide you through all the levels of emotion down to the love. It also helps if your therapist isn't suppressing his emotions either, and can share and express his own feelings freely.

Telling the truth doesn't mean you should go around dumping your negative feelings.

What You Feel You Can Heal

By fully feeling your emotions and expressing the complete truth about them, you will be able to heal the unresolved emotional tension and be free to love more fully. Feeling your emotions and expressing them is the means to releasing them. However, this doesn't mean you should go out and 'dump' all your negativity on your loved ones. Going out and indiscriminately sharing all your feelings could ruin your relationships and create even more trauma for you to deal with.

Sharing Feelings Is Not Easy

In the beginning, telling the complete truth might be difficult and even painful, especially when it would be so much easier to just take a nap or forget all about it. But in the long run, it is your only hope. Telling the complete truth means admitting doubt when you would rather pretend certainty, talking about your feelings when you would rather pout, asking for what you want when you'd rather pretend everything's fine, admitting you made a mistake when you would rather blame someone else, and sharing your hurt and sadness when you'd rather stop caring.

Many times its easier to tell a "little while lie" but in the long run telling the truth is your only hope.

Using Tact

There is an art to telling the truth which you will develop after lots of practice. It is called TACT.

Telling the
Absolute
Complete
Truth

Whenever you use TACT, your ability to experience love will increase. By using TACT, you can express your feelings so they can be healed rather than become intensified. The expression of emotion with TACT will leave you feeling more loving, clear and alive.

In the following chapters you will learn to express the complete truth without making your relationships crazy.

Telling the Absolute Complete Truth

Chapter 7

What Makes Relationships So Crazy?

The information in this chapter contains one of the most important discoveries I have made about relationships and has already changed the lives of thousands of people we've taught. In the previous chapters, we've seen how your own repressed feelings will affect your behavior. But there is one amazing phenomenon that we've overlooked. It's a phenomenon that I've observed in every family and every intimate relationship. It occurs in varying degrees according to how intimate you have become with another person.

I call this law of behavior the **See-Saw Effect.**

The See-Saw Effect explains why the more calm and detached a husband becomes, the more hysterical and panicky his wife gets. It explains why nice, even-tempered people may tend to attract partners who appear to have violent tempers. It explains why a strong, stable woman might start a relationship with a man and suddenly find herself feeling insecure and needy.

In short, the See-Saw Effect offers an understanding of the mechanics of human interaction that explains what makes relationships so crazy.

The See-Saw Effect explains why the more calm and detached a husband becomes, the more upset his wife becomes.

Your Emotional Connection

To begin, imagine two containers of liquid, like tanks standing upright, as in the illustration. We'll connect the two tanks with a pipe or tube, so that if we wish, we can transfer liquid from one tank to another. In our analogy, those tanks represent two people in a relationship: Fred and Wilma, for instance. The liquid in the tanks represents our emotions. And the connecting tube represents that sensitivity to one another they feel as husband and wife.

You develop that connection with another person under certain circumstances — when you are family members, when you live together, when you are close business partners and, most importantly, when you have sex with someone. That emotional connection allows you to share in what the other person is feeling. It's responsible for your knowing your partner is angry at you, even if he or she denies it and for a child knowing his Mommy is mad, even though she tells him nothing is wrong.

The more connected you are to another person, the more you are able to share and experience their feelings.

When two people fall in love,
their emotional connection allows
them to share each other's feelings.

What You Suppress
Your Partner Will Express

Now, let's look at how the energy flows between these two containers. Something happens to Wilma and she begins to experience the emotion of anger. Imagine anger as a liquid emotion beginning to rise up in her tank. But when Wilma was growing up, she was taught that nice girls don't get angry — men don't like angry women. Wilma can feel her hurt and sadness, but doesn't have permission to feel her anger. So, without even realizing it, Wilma automatically begins to push down her anger, to **Repress** it. A little voice inside of her says: "calm down, Wilma, there's nothing to get angry about."

As Wilma pushes and pushes her anger down, a very strange thing happens — it goes over to the other side of the tank. All of a sudden, Fred starts to get irritable and angry. The more upset and angry he becomes, the more Wilma tries to calm him down. She tries to repress his angry feelings just as she has tried to repress hers. This continues until Fred just explodes. And Wilma will say to herself: "I just can't understand why he loses control like that. I guess men have hot tempers."

When Wilma pushes down her anger, Fred feels it and becomes angry. What you suppress your partner will express.

***When we push down a feeling, it comes up in our partner.
This is what we call the See-Saw Effect.***

The principle of the See-Saw Effect is:

What you suppress, your partner may express.

And of course, the reverse:

What your partner suppresses, you may express.

This principle really is the physics of relationships, explaining how your emotions affect your partner's and how your partner's emotions affect yours. In the case we just saw, Wilma was suppressing her anger and Fred began expressing it.

Here's how the See-Saw Effect works with another level of emotion — fear and insecurity. Fred starts to become afraid. Maybe he is working on a new book and is afraid it won't turn out the way he wants.

Trying to remain cool and collected by suppressing his own fears, Fred is unknowingly fueling the fires of Wilma's fear.

Maybe he is expanding his business and is afraid of the financial risks. But Fred was taught while growing up that as a man he should be strong and confident. Men don't get afraid — they just forge ahead. And they certainly don't ever show anyone they are afraid. So, what does Fred do with that emotion of fear? That's right, he suppresses it, unconsciously pushing it down in his tank.

The more Fred pushes down his fear, the more it goes over onto Wilma's side. All of a sudden, Wilma starts to feel insecure, fearful and panicky. She will probably start to express her fears and as Fred hears her express her fear, he will resist her even more and say: "Honey, there's nothing to worry about. Calm down." As Fred gets more and more detached and unfeeling, Wilma will feel her fears intensify until she becomes quite panicky and almost hysterical with worry. Fred suppresses his fears and Wilma expresses them.

This becomes a vicious circle, because the more afraid and nervous Wilma becomes, the more Fred tries to remain cool, calm and collected by suppressing his own fears. Fred is unknowingly fueling the fire of Wilma's hysteria by trying to remain in control.

Why Women May Seem Overemotional

I've seen this pattern happen over and over again with women who can't understand why they become so insecure and hysterical around the men they love and men who can't understand why otherwise logical and strong women seem to fall apart around them. The answer is the See-Saw Effect. The men are following their conditioning to not show feelings of fear and the women end up expressing all the men's suppressed fearful emotion. The extreme case of this is the controlling, even-tempered husband, never expressing any emotion that could be taken for weakness or self-doubt, driving the wife into overemotionalism and hysteria, then making the woman feel inferior and mentally ill by constantly pointing out how emotional she is becoming. Many women literally end up in mental institutions when this happens to them over a long period of time. And of course, there are cases of the reverse: women controlling themselves and the men exploding with feelings.

Even-tempered men can easily drive women into hysteria.

Why Women May Become "Needy"

Let's take one more example of the See-Saw Effect: the emotion of "need". Fred and Wilma fall in love and as they become closer, Fred starts to feel his need for Wilma. But that feeling frightens him, because if he needs her, he could lose her. So Fred pushes down his feelings of need, telling himself he doesn't want to get too close or committed. What happens to his need when he pushes it down? Right — it goes over to Wilma's side of the tank, adding to her own feelings of need and blowing them out of proportion. Wilma starts to feel what is commonly called "needy". She becomes very afraid of losing Fred and she feels desperate to get a commitment from him; she feels weak in his presence.

The more Fred suppresses his needs, the more needy Wilma feels. When Fred sees her feeling needy, he will naturally resist her. The more he resists his own needs being mirrored back to him, the stronger they will get in Wilma.

This phenomenon is very common in intimate relationships. Some men go from one woman to another, wondering why they all become so needy around them. What they don't realize is that each woman is reflecting the man's own needs back to him, needs he is afraid to look at and feel.

Some people go from one partner to another, wondering why they all become so "needy" and insecure.

How The See-Saw Effect Blows Your Feelings Out Of Proportion

Does all this mean that every time you feel angry, it isn't really your anger — it's your husband's? Or, if you walk into work and yell at your secretary, it is really she who is angry? Not at all. Don't use this information to prove that you are right and someone else is wrong.

Let's look at the See-Saw Effect a little more closely. Wilma and Fred go to a restaurant and wait a half an hour to be served. Let's say they each feel a little annoyed and angry — 10% angry, for instance. But Fred's conditioning tells him it is not OK to be angry, especially about small things, so he pushes it down. The See-Saw Effect takes over, and now Wilma is feeling 20% angry and annoyed. Fred notices her feeling angry and tries to calm her down. The more he pushes down his feelings, the more her feelings will intensify. She was angry also — it's not all Fred's anger she is expressing, but now her anger and annoyance in the restaurant will be way out of proportion.

By being nice and suppressing your annoyance, your partner's annoyance will intensify.

Mirror, Mirror On The Wall

You may be starting to understand why you sometimes feel crazy in relationships. Have you ever noticed that you try to do everything to calm your partner down and he or she just gets more and more upset? That's because your partner is probably expressing an emotion that you are suppressing. People close to you will act like mirrors, reflecting back to you a perfect image of yourself, including the parts of yourself you would rather not look at or deal with. So, if you are suppressing your fears, your partner may continue to pester you with her fears and worries, as if to hold a mirror up to you and say: "Hey, take a look at some of the feelings you are pushing down."

So, something else important to realize is:

You will resist in your partner what you suppress in yourself.

If Fred is suppressing his anger, not wanting to deal with it, and it goes over into Wilma's tanks, she will start to get angry. When he sees her anger, what is his natural reaction? He will try and suppress her anger also. Fred will resist seeing in Wilma what he is pushing down in himself. Trying to change your partner's emotions or talk them out of feeling a feeling is a sure sign that they are mirroring to you an emotion you don't want to feel in yourself.

If you are resisting your partner's emotions, it's probably because you are resisting those same emotions within yourself.

You will resist in your partner what you suppress in yourself.

When one parent suppresses negative emotions, the other may uncontrollably express those emotions.

The See-Saw Effect And Your Parents

Think back to your childhood. Did you have one parent who was the "good guy", the nice parent, the one who seemed to be the victim of the other, and one parent who was the "bad guy", the one who got angry, yelled, did the disciplining? Now that you understand the See-Saw Effect, think again — perhaps your nice parent was suppressing so much anger and resentment that the other parent had to constantly express it in order to try and dissolve some of the tension. When one parent pushes down negative emotions in himself or herself, the other parent will inevitably express those emotions.

Kids And The See-Saw Effect

The See-Saw Effect occurs quite dramatically in families with children. We can redefine the principle and say:

What you suppress, your children may express.

Many parents think they should hide their feelings from their children in order to protect or shelter them. I feel this couldn't be farther from the truth. Your children will pick up your feelings anyway, whether you choose to express them consciously or not, and the kids will only feel confused by the mixed messages and may even start feeling that they are responsible for making you unhappy.

What you suppress, your children may express.

If a parent is suppressing anger and hostility towards his spouse, for instance, the children will express it and act it out through angry, rebellious behavior and temper tantrums. If a parent is suppressing his sadness and hurt, the children will cry more. If a parent is pushing down his feelings of fear and insecurity, the children may whine and become more fearful.

This is why it's essential to work together as a family solving the family problems. There's no such thing as one person having a problem that is theirs alone when that person lives with others.

The Multiple Tank Effect

Let's take a look at what happens when there are more than just two people in a relationship. Fred is married to Wilma. What Fred doesn't know is that Wilma is having an affair with Barney. So now, we have three tanks connected. Barney is also married to Betty. So there are four tanks, four sets of emotions involved.

One day, Betty feels sad because she feels Barney pulling away, but she suppresses her feelings since she wants to be a good wife. What she suppresses, Barney starts to feel, but he is a man (a cave man to boot!) so he suppresses his feelings too. What he suppresses, Wilma starts to feel. She adds her own suppressed sadness, pushes all of it down and it passes on to Fred. One morning, Fred wakes up feeling very sad and depressed, and he doesn't even know Betty, who started it all in the first place.

Multiple relationships can get extremely complicated. It's hard enough to balance the emotional energies between two people, let alone three or four. This is one of the problems with open relationships and affairs — they confuse the emotional balance between partners.

It's hard enough to balance the emotional energies of two people, let alone three or even four.

When the emotional connection is broken, a relationship loses its liveliness and excitement.

Breaking The Connection

What happens when both people in a relationship suppress their feelings, when both sides of the tank are being pushed down? All the pressure goes into that connecting pipe, and it eventually bursts. This is what occurs in many relationships. Neither party tells the complete truth about their feelings; they push down their emotions, drift apart, and eventually break their emotional connection entirely. They have successfully repressed all feelings for one another.

This is what causes you to feel you have fallen out of love with someone, that you have lost your attraction — it's just that the connection is broken. Two people can live comfortably together, if they choose to, once they have broken the connection, because the source of tension will be gone. They will no longer be victims of the See-Saw Effect. But they have lost the love, the passion and the aliveness in the relationship. And more importantly, they have lost the opportunity to grow and learn from the mirror of their partner.

It is possible to mend those broken emotional pipes, but it takes a lot of work and diligent practice of the techniques in the next section of this book.

How To Recognize The See-Saw Effect

If you notice your partner, parent, child, etc. expressing some emotions — anger, fear, sadness, need — and you begin to feel annoyed, irritated or resistant to them, they are probably expressing some of what you are suppressing inside. Because you resist your emotions, you will resist your partner's similar emotions.

If you are resisting your partner's emotions, it's probably because you are resisting those same emotions within yourself.

On the other hand, if your partner expresses a feeling and you don't feel annoyed or irritated and can easily confort them, you are probably not suppressing any emotions, and they are simply expressing their own feelings.

When you feel irritated by your partner's feelings, they are probably expressing what you are suppressing.

You can't avoid the See-Saw Effect but you can use it to grow and create more love in your life.

What You Can Do About The See-Saw Effect

You can't get rid of the See-Saw Effect — it is a dynamic of human interaction which is a part of any relationship. You **can** prevent yourself and others from unnecessary anguish and hurt by doing the following:

1. Start taking responsibility for your emotions — express them instead of suppressing them.

2. When someone close to you is expressing an emotion and you notice yourself resisting them, stop and ask yourself: Are they expressing something I am not willing to experience or look at in myself?

3. When you notice your feelings and your intimate partner's feelings are intensifying by the minute, don't go any further until you practice some of the techniques in the next chapter.

Chapter 8

The Heart Techniques

The techniques in the following section of this book have assisted thousands of people in learning to dissolve their emotional tensions and resolve the inevitable conflicts of relationships. If if weren't for these techniques, thousands of couples I have worked with wouldn't be loving and cooperating — not because they don't love each other, but because the tensions and conflicts of being in an intimate relationship or of ending an intimate relationship would be too much to handle. Understanding why you are fighting (the See Saw Effect and the Four R's) is great, *but it is not enough.* Knowing what to do about it and how to resolve the tension and come back to loving is what will really enrich your relationships and keep them working.

I suggest you practice everything described in this chapter on a daily basis. You may ask, "Why do I need to use these techniques if I don't feel I have big problems?" The answer is that by using these techniques, the little, every day tensions won't build up and develop into major problems. The moment you notice tension or resistence building in your relationships, or any lessening of feeling fully connected, these techniques and skills can be used in order to prevent the emotional separation from expanding and coming between you and your loved ones. Taking care of your relationships consistently will keep them healthy, and support you in staying in touch with your inner positive feelings — love, confidence and happiness.

The moment you feel slight resistance to the other person, this is the time to put the problem aside and practice one of the following Heart Techniques:

1. The Duplication Technique
2. The Anger Process
3. the Love Letter Technique

The Duplication Technique

The first technique to begin practicing in your relationships is called "Duplication." This technique is based on the principle that:

Duplication dissolves tension and creates connection

Duplication is not really foreign to you. It is one of the basic ways you learned many skills while growing up. Remember learning to ride a bike? If your father had given you instructions, or shown you a a book about bike riding, you probably would have been too scared to learn. Instead, he got on the bike and showed you how to ride. Part of your learning process was duplicating him, doing just what he did. You learned how to speak through duplicating your parents. Your Mother said, "Say 'mama,' " and eventually you duplicated her voice and said "mama". In response to your attempt, you felt closer to her and felt more of her love and acceptance of you.

Whenever another person duplicates how you are feeling, you will feel relieved. This one principle is probably responsible for the success of all soap operas and horror films. If you are feeling sad and depressed and you watch someone on TV feeling sad and depressed, you will actually experience feeling better. They duplicate your sadness, and that helps dissolve the emotional tension. Horror films are popular because you watch other people being scared out of their minds, and in a sense, they are duplicating your own fears of pain, death and the unknown.

How Duplication Works

You can use the Duplication Technique in relationships to dissolve the emotional tension between yourself and a partner/child/parent/friend, etc. Simply, when you notice the tension building up between you, you each take turns duplicating how the other person is feeling. Just having someone outside of yourself express your own feelings, creates a release and allows you to go to deeper levels of acceptance and clarity.

Here's how Duplication works:

Fred and Wilma are discussing a new project. They are building a new art gallery in Los Angeles, and have hired a contractor who is giving them a lot of trouble and is behind schedule. Both Fred and Wilma are worried about the project not being completed on time.

Fred, however, is suppressing some of his anxiety and fear, taking the role of the strong male, and Wilma is expressing her own worries and feeling his as well. It's the See Saw Effect. But, none of this matters, because...

It's a waste of time to try and figure out who started an argument or who is suppressing and who is expressing. All that is important is to dissolve the emotional tension and reconnect through duplication.

Here is Fred and Wilma's conversation, leading into an argument:

Wilma: Honey, I just talked to the contractor, and he said he still doesn't have the carpeting in. Not only that, he doesn't even know where the lights are.

Fred: What do you mean, he doesn't know where the lights are?

Wilma: They haven't even arrived. They are on some truck somewhere, and it's been two weeks since they left the factory. I am really starting to get worried.

Fred: Look, don't worry about it, O.K.?

Wilma: Well, I am worried. What if the lights don't come in time? What if we have our open house and it looks awful?

Fred: Stop panicking! It will all work out. Worrying won't do anything *(getting annoyed).*

Wilma: Maybe we just went in over our heads. Maybe we can't take all this new responsibility — it's so much work. Why can't you see how I feel?

Fred: I'm taking care of everything. It's been my project all along, so just trust me and shut up.

Wilma: I do trust you, but...

Fred: You don't trust me. You just keep nagging about the stupid lights. Let's forget it.

Wilma: I can't forget it and stop shouting at me.

Fred: You know what your problem is? You can't trust me. You are just messed up. *(Fred has blown a fuse himself)*

Fred and Wilma are now off and running with a full blown fight. If they continue to argue, they will both blow up, or repress the whole issue and create deep resentment between them. The solution is for them to stop verbally fighting, and practice the *Duplication Technique* to dissolve the emotional tension.

The Duplication Technique allows you to feel and to release your resistence. In the beginning, it may be uncomfortable to duplicate your

140

partner and you may not want to practice Duplication, since it is their feelings that you are resisting.

By going ahead and practicing Duplication, you will burn through your resistence and, as a result, feel closer to your partner and also assist them in feeling better.

So, remember, the more you resist doing the technique, the more you need to practice it and the better you will feel afterwards.

How to Practice Duplication

Part A. Giving Lines

1. Whenever you notice you are beginning to resist your partner (child, roommate, etc.), you ask the other person for permission to practice Duplication.
2. One person goes first. If it is you, for instance, you ask your partner to express his or her feelings to you one line at a time, and you repeat back to them exactly what they say. Act as if you are the other person. Don't imitate or make fun of what they say, just play their role.
3. The person giving the lines should try and express the complete truth about how they are feeling as discussed in previous chapters (starting with anger and moving through hurt, fear, guilt and love). In many cases though, it is enough to express a few of your emotions and then some positive feelings.
4. As you listen to your partner's lines and repeat them back, you will start getting a clear idea of just how they must feel, and you will be able to add your own lines which appropriately express how they are feeling. At this point your partner will begin to feel relieved, and see that you actually do understand how they are feeling.

Part B. Owning Your Partners Feelings

1. When your partner finishes, then you duplicate their feelings and viewpoint without being given lines. You don't have to agree with their point of view to understand it or to feel what they are feeling. Imagine that you have become them and temporarily "own" their feelings and thoughts. Express back to them all their feelings, get into it and you will find yourself supporting them and even adding new complaints. Sometimes you may still need a little prompting.

This is O.K. but your intention in Step B is to duplicate without "lines."

2. In the beginning, you will probably feel a resistance to repeating the lines back to your partner. Just continue, and as you connect more with your partners feelings through duplicating them out loud, the tension will dissove, and it will feel easier and easier to say what they are feeling.

*Note: If after 3 or 4 minutes it doesn't become easier to repeat your partner's feelings, to mirror them back, and you start feeling very upset and angry, your conflict has developed beyond the point of surface tension, and duplication **will not** work. In this case, you need to use the Love Letter technique described later in this chapter.*

Part C. Switching

When one person is finished duplicating their partner's feelings, the couple should switch, and the one who repeated the lines now gets a turn to give lines expressing his feelings to the other person for them to repeat back.

A Sample of Duplication

Part A. Giving Lines.

Wilma gives Fred lines expressing how she feels, and he duplicates each one back to her, without any wise cracks, comments, explanations, or defense statements. Fred will probably feel like making comments but must not, otherwise the technique doesn't work. He will have his turn later.

Note: Wilma may have a lot of emotion in her voice when she gives Fred her lines, but he may repeat them back without much feeling, especially at first. That's fine — as he continues to repeat back how she is feeling, as if he is Wilma, he will begin to get in touch with his own feelings and will become more animated.

Here's an example:

Wilma: I am just fed up with that contractor.

Fred: *(Duplicating her lines)* I am just fed up with that contractor.

Wilma: What a jerk! Now he says he even lost our lighting system.

Fred: What a jerk! Now he says he even lost our lighting system.

Wilma: What if they never arrive? What if our open house comes and we have no lights?

Fred: What if they never arrive? What if our open house comes and we have no lights?

Wilma: I am really worried. Maybe we got in over our heads.

Fred: I am really worried. Maybe we got in over our heads.

Wilma: And I feel really hurt that you don't understand how worried I am.

Fred: And I feel really hurt that you don't understand how worried I am.

Wilma: You always act so cool and calm and let me worry about things. You make me feel foolish.

Fred: You always act so cool and calm and let me worry about things. You make me feel foolish.

Wilma: Well, I am scared that we will just fail.

Fred: Well, I am scared that we will just fail. I am scared that the place will look awful. *(Fred is starting to add some of his own lines now, as he sees how Wilma feels and is starting to get in touch with his own feelings).*

Wilma: Yeah, me too, I'm scared the place will look awful. Now I'd like you to duplicate me without lines.

Part B Owning Your Partner's Feelings

When Wilma asks Fred to duplicate without lines, she may already be feeling much better or maybe not; it doesn't matter — Part B will take care of that. However, Fred may start getting upset but before he has his turn to express his feelings he must "own" and duplicate Wilma's feelings for a least a minute or two. Here's an example of Fred acting as if he is Wilma:

Fred: "I'm so worried about the gallery being ready on time. What if we don't get the lights installed before the opening? It would be a disaster. I hate that irresponsible contractor. And I hate you for acting so cool and detached like nothing is wrong. I resent you looking at me like I'm over-emotional. You look like Robot-man. You make me feel foolish. It hurts my feelings when you act so indifferent to my feelings. I want you to care about my feelings. I want you to comfort me and express your feelings too. I love you so much; you are so wonderful."

At this point, Wilma will feel much better because her feelings are being shared by Fred. Fred will feel at least less resistant because he has at least accepted, heard and felt Wilma's feelings. Duplicating Wilma's feelings will have probably stirred up some feelings in Fred and he will now need Wilma to duplicate him. (However, this is not always the case; both Wilma and Fred may already be feeling resolved and they won't need to switch).

Part C: Switching

This step is optional. If Fred feels any roughness or tension, then he will need to have Wilma duplicate him. They then begin the process all over again doing both Part A and Part B. Here's an example of Fred and Wilma switching;

Part A

Fred: I hate you for always panicking.
Wilma: I hate you for always panicking.
Fred: I already knew the lights were late.
Wilma: I already knew the lights were late.
Fred: I hate when you don't trust me.
Wilma: I hate when you don't trust me.
Fred: When you panic, it makes me feel really upset. Why do you have to panic?
Wilma: When you panic, it makes me feel really upset. Why do you have to panic?
Fred: I feel attacked by you.
Wilma: I feel attacked by you.
Fred: I feel you don't believe in me.
Wilma: I feel you don't believe in me.
Fred: It hurts me to see you so upset.
Wilma: It hurts me to see you so upset.
Fred: I want you to trust me.
Wilma: I want you to trust me.
Fred: I want you to believe in me.
Wilma: I want you to believe in me.
Fred: I want you to think I am great.
Wilma: I want you to think I am great.
Fred: I want you to feel happy and safe.
Wilma: I want you to feel happy and safe.
Fred: It upsets me when you get upset.
Wilma: It upsets me when you get upset.
Fred: I love you so much. I think you are wonderful. I can also understand your feelings. I'm a little nervous too.
Wilma: I love you so much. I think you are wonderful. I can also understand your feelings. I'm a little nervous too.

145

Here's an example of Wilma as she owns Freds feelings and gives them back without "lines". Wilma pretends that she is Fred and expresses his feelings.

Part B

Wilma: Why do you have to panic about everything? You're never happy. You always worry. Don't you trust me? Just relax, will you; everything will turn out OK. I hate it when I work hard and you don't believe in me. It really hurts. It makes me sad when you don't trust me. Sometimes you are such a nag. I want you to love and support me and not criticize me. I want you to love me, I deserve it. I'm wonderful and you're wonderful too!

One of the greatest values of the Duplication Technique is that it offers you an opportunity to verbally express your feelings without the other person constantly making comments and resisting what you are saying. If I start out expressing my feelings to my partner, she will naturally feel compelled to interrupt me and disagree and this interferes with my process of working through those five levels of emotions.

Here is another example of Duplication:

The Incident:

One day Fred calls up Wilma's mother to ask a question and forgets who he is calling for a moment, so that when Wilma's mother answers the phone, he doesn't remember her name. They talk for a few minutes and then he gets off the phone. Wilma notices herself feeling really annoyed with Fred. Here is how their fight would normally unfold:

Wilma: Fred, I thought you were really rude to my mother.

Fred: Rude? I wasn't rude.

Wilma: You were rude; you forgot her name. How could you forget my mother's name? She must have felt awful.

Fred: Don't make such a big deal about it. I can't always remember everyone's name.

Wilma: My mother is not "everyone". Sometimes I think you don't have any brains.

Fred: Look, I didn't want to call her in the first place; it was your idea. I'm never calling her again.

Wilma: Don't threaten me. Stop acting like a baby.

Fred: You are so critical. You make me sick...

STOP!!!!

146

Without Duplication, this discussion will quickly escalate into name calling, door slamming and separation. If you read back over the dialogue, you will see that in Wilma's second sentence, she is starting to get in touch with her hurt feelings for her mother, but Fred interrupts the natural process and expresses his anger, thus stimulating more anger in Wilma. Fred and Wilma will stay stuck in anger until they get too tired to fight anymore or just suppress the whole thing. Watch how Duplication helps:

Wilma: I am really irritated at you about that phone call. I want you to duplicate me.

Fred: OK.

Wilma: What are you, some kind of dumbbell, forgetting my mother's name?

Fred: What are you, some kind of dumbbell, forgetting my mother's name?

Wilma: How could you be so rude to my mother?

Fred: How could you be so rude to my mother?

Wilma: I feel so hurt for her; she must feel awful.

Fred: I feel so hurt for her; she must feel awful.

Wilma: Yeah, her son-in-law calls and doesn't even know her name.

Fred: (Starting to connect with Wilma's feelings) Yeah, her son-in-law calls and acts like a jerk, doesn't even remember her name.

Wilma: My mother loves you so much and she must feel awful and rejected.

Fred: My mother loves you so much and she must feel awful and rejected.

Wilma: I want you to love my mother; I want you to care about my family.

Fred: I want you to love my mother; I want you to care about my family and show that you care about me too.

Wilma: That's right, I want you to love me more too.

At this point, both Wilma and Fred see that what was really upsetting her was not that she thought that she had a stupid husband, but that she felt hurt that he didn't care about her family. Fred can now understand her feelings and remedy the situation. And naturally, as Fred duplicates Wilma saying he is stupid for forgetting her mother's name, he is expressing his own feelings that perhaps his pride wouldn't allow him to express before. What could have turned into a big argument becomes an opportunity to feel closer with one another. Fred then completes the process by doing Part B (duplicating without lines).

Here's an example of Fred owning Wilma's feelings:

Fred: What kind of an idiot are you anyway? Don't you have any brains? You make me sick. You are so self-centered. How could you forget my mother's name. That really hurts. I bet it really hurt her too. How would you feel? Sometimes you are so insensitive. I hate your petty excuses. I wish you would care more about people and not get so spaced out. I feel sad that you forgot my mother's name. She must have felt awful. I want you to love my mother and my family. I want you to really care. I want you to show how much you really care. I love you so much and I forgive you... but don't do it again.

In this example Fred has actually expressed more anger at himself than Wilma did. This will not only make Fred feel better but allow Wilma to more fully forgive and love him again.

What To Do When You Don't Know What You Are Feeling

If you are experiencing tension between you and your partner and want to express your feelings with Duplication but aren't sure what those feelings are, try using "lead-in phrases." One good lead-in phrase is: "Right now I am feeling..." and just fill in the blank without editing what comes up. By repeating this over and over and simply completing the sentence, you will move through your block and your feelings will begin to flow again.

Example: I am feeling irritated with my partner and I want to practice the Duplication technique but I am not sure how to express what I am feeling to him. Instead of just saying: "I don't know how I feel", which is sure to frustrate him, I say:

Right now I am feeling... stuck.

Right now I am feeling... frustrated.

Right now I am feeling... like I just want to hide.

Right now I am feeling... like you don't care.

Right now I am feeling... hurt that you didn't like the speech I wrote. Sometimes you act like you take me for granted. It makes me feel awful." etc.

148

As I went through the exercise, I began to get in touch with my real feelings. If I get stuck again, I will repeat the lead-in phrase and practice "sentence completion" until the feelings start flowing freely again. When you use this technique to get unstuck, make sure your partner duplicates each line you say.

How To Use Duplication With Family, Friends, And In Business

The Duplication technique works well in any kind of relationship — parent/child, brother/sister, employer/employee, between friends or roomates. If you are single, for instance, and you are feeling irritated at someone in your life who is not around to practice these techniques with, you just ask a friend to practice Duplication with you.

Example: Wilma is really furious at her boss. He kept her late at work again last night and the next day he doesn't even thank her. She comes home from work and stomps around the apartment, feeling miserable. Wilma has two choices: she can hold onto that tension and anger or she can ask a roommate or friend to practice Duplication.

Wilma will pretend she is talking to her boss, and one line at a time will express all of her feelings while her friend duplicates back each line.

Wilma: Mr. Simpson, you are a total jerk.
Friend: Mr. Simpson, you are a total jerk.
Wilma: You have no respect for me at all and I am fed up with it.
Friend: You have no respect for me at all and I am fed up with it.
Wilma: I feel awful when you treat me like a piece of furniture.
Friend: I feel awful when you treat me like a piece of furniture.
Wilma: I guess I am really hurt that you don't show more interest in me and appreciate me more, etc.

Wilma accomplishes several things by practicing Duplication. First, she releases some of the physical and emotional tension by expressing her feelings rather than keeping them suppressed inside. Second, by expressing her feelings in this way, she was able to work down through to what was really bothering her — that she wasn't feeling appreciated — rather than staying stuck in feelings of anger and blame. And third, Wilma avoided building up her stockpile of anger and resentment and then dumping it inappropriately on some innocent bystander.

More Examples

You can even use the Duplication technique with someone who doesn't know you are practicing it at the time. A very well known TV Director named Bill attended one of my HEART seminars and learned all of the techniques in this chapter. A few days later, he was on the set and became very angry with a crew member. Without thinking, he yelled at the crew member in front of the whole cast, humiliating the man and creating a tremendous amount of tension on the set. The next day when Bill came into work, the crew member was furious at him and the entire cast was irritable and nervous.

Bill decided to try out the Duplication technique. He called the crew member over and in private began duplicating his feelings. "You know," Bill said, "when I yelled at you yesterday in front of everyone, I bet you probably felt like saying to me: "How dare you yell at me in front of the whole cast. Don't you have any sense of respect for my position here? Who are you anyway to make a scene Mr. Big Shot Director." The crew member looked astonished that Bill was expressing all of his resentment and began to smile. Bill continued: "And you know, if I were you, I'd probably feel really hurt that the director didn't seem to care about my feelings and I would be afraid our relationship was ruined forever." The crew member nodded enthusiastically and answered: "Yes, that's exactly how I felt." "Well, I'm sorry," Bill apologized, "I just wasn't thinking. I really understand how bad it made you feel." "I believe you really do understand," the crew member answered and the two shook hands.

When Bill told us that story, he said that after he practiced Duplication with the crew member, the change on the set was remarkable — people were laughing, the cast got along beautifully and they finished their work early that day. No one even knew what Bill had done, but they could all feel the release of tension. If Bill had just said: "I'm sorry," and the crew member would have answered: "that's OK," things would have been fine but only on the surface. By practicing Duplication, Bill allowed the emotional release to come from a deeper level and showed the crew member that his feelings were really understood.

Sally used Duplication with her six year old son, Brian. Brian was supposed to go to a friend's house for the weekend, but something came up and Sally couldn't drive him there. Brian stormed around the house and started fighting with his little sister. Sally decided to practice Duplication on Brian. So she decided to duplicate how she thought he must feel. "You know, Brian, if I were you I would be thinking: 'Boy, Mom is just so mean. I hate her. She is the worst mom in the world. She promises to do something with me, and she goes back on it. This is the worst weekend of my life. I never have any fun." As Sally expressed what she thought her son was feeling inside, Brian started to cry and began to release and experience his own emotion. His mother expressed all of his suppressed feelings and he felt a relief.

Duplication is not simply a fancy technique for understanding the other person's point of view, but is an opportunity to resolve stored up emotional tension, to tell the complete truth and to connect yourself with another person on a deep emotional level. We all need to feel that someone else really understands how we are feeling. Duplication fulfills this natural human need and allows you to resolve the inner emotional tension and release undesirable emotions like frustration, anxiety and depression.

The Anger Process

The Anger Process is a simple, yet profoundly effective technique for releasing anger and preventing self-hate and guilt. Whenever you get angry about something, it is due to the frustration of your desire to get or possess something. You can easily release some of the tension around anger and frustration by recognizing and expressing the desire or intention which is being frustrated.

By first fully expressing your anger and blame, you can then feel and express what it is you wanted or expected. By feeling and expressing what you want, very naturally you will begin to feel that part of you that knows: "I deserve to get what I want." Underneath all anger is desire and underneath desire is a feeling of self-love and worthiness.
The following is a helpful graph mapping out the origins of anger:

ANGER/BLAME

I DIDN'T GET

I WANT

I DESERVE

I AM
(Self-love, Self-worth, Inner Strength)

The anger process is a way to retrace your steps and turn your anger into the positive force that it really is at its source. You can now see from the graph the obvious consequences of suppressing or bottling up your anger. When you deny your feelings of anger, you automatically begin to lose touch with your natural wants and desires. Then, as you become numb to your wants, you automatically begin to deny your natural innate feelings of self-worth, self-love and self-esteem. By denying your anger, you deny its source, which is your true source of strength, power and confidence.

To fully regain your inner power, you can use the Anger Process and feel better in a matter of minutes. The Anger Process has three steps:

153

Step One — Getting Angry at Yourself

Whenever you make a mistake, miss an opportunity or disappoint yourself, use this "upset" as an opportunity to get angry at yourself. Begin the process by looking in the mirror and getting angry at yourself.

Use phrases like:

"I resent you for... "
"I hate you for..."
"You make me sick when..."
"I don't like it when..."
"You embarrassed me when..."

Begin to verbalize out loud all the possible rational or irrational blame and anger that you can come up with. You may find yourself yelling and screaming or you may just use an angry or firm, deliberate tone. (NOTE: By screaming at the top of your lungs, you can easily lose touch with the real feelings—screaming can be a way of avoiding your real feelings).

Be sure to use "You" statements and not "I" statements. This allows the anger to get out and not be held in. For example:

DON'T SAY:	DO SAY:
I hate myself	I hate you
I am so bad	You are so bad
I am sick of being weak	I am so sick of YOUR weakness
I hate being a wimp	I hate when you wimp out

After 2 to 3 minutes of unedited and even exaggerated anger and blame, then move on to Step Two.

Step Two — Becoming the Motivator

In Step Two, you now become your own motivator. Maintaining the same angry, assertive energy in your voice, begin motivating yourself by saying what you want and don't want. For example:

I want you to be more responsible.
I don't want you to give up so soon.
Stop acting like a wimp.
Grow up, will you?
I want you to really put yourself out there.
I want you to succeed.
I want you to feel good about yourself.
I want you to stop complaining all the time.
etc.

After a minute or two of expressing your desires and intentions, move onto Step Three.

Step Three — Becoming Your Own Cheerleader and Fan Club

Using the same firm tone of voice, continue expressing your feelings by using positive, supportive statements. For example:

You can do it.
You deserve to succeed.
You deserve to be respected.
You are wonderful!
You are great!
I love your courage and strength.
I think you are the greatest.
I love you.
You will be successful.
Everyone likes you because you are such a real loving person.

In summary,
the Anger Process has three steps;

Step 1 — Express Anger and Blame.
(Use "you" statements —
direct the anger out)

Step 2 — Express what you want.
(Use "I want" statements)

Step 3 — Express positive, loving,
supportive statements.

When and How to Practice
the Anger Process

Whenever you are feeling down, somewhere in your subconscious you are blaming yourself. The anger allows you to bring those feelings up and out and then bring out the inner love and power. **This process can be even more effective if you do it with a partner.** To do it with a partner, imagine that your partner is you and begin expressing your anger and blame. Your partner then duplicates back every sentence.

The powerful and energizing result of this process can only be experienced; it can't be described or imagined. The next time you want to feel better, more awake, more alive, more powerful or more expressive, then find something about yourself at which to get angry. If you can't find anything, make up something or remember something from your past. If you are in a situation where it is inappropriate to express such feelings, you can write them out. Some people tape the Anger Process and play it on their way to work, duplicating back every sentence. Remember, when you make the recording, leave space to duplicate back.

This process can be easily taught to all your friends. To teach them, give a brief explanation and then simply demonstrate it to them and have them duplicate each line.

Another side benefit of having a friend (spouse, etc) duplicate your anger is that if they have any anger towards you it will get released and they will feel much closer to you.

When anyone feels resistance and tension in my office, we all practice the Anger Process together. In this case, the whole staff duplicates for the person getting angry at themselves.

3

The
Love Letter
Technique...

The Love Letter Technique

The Love Letter Technique is the ultimate technique for sharing and expressing the complete truth for resolving emotional conflict both within yourself and in your relationships. It is not only a powerful tool for emotional healing, but through practicing it, you will learn more about your own feelings and about what it really means to tell the truth.

In the past five years thousands of people have attended my seminars and have successfully learned to practice the Love Letter Technique. Heart graduates report that in a matter of minutes, they are able to resolve emotional conflicts that would otherwise seem impossible and get repressed.

159

The Love Letter Format

To write a Love Letter, begin by expressing your anger, resentment and blame and allow yourself to move through the other levels until you get down to the love.

Each Love Letter has five parts — and the following lead-in phrases may help you if you get stuck in one level and need to move into the next.

1. Anger and Blame

I don't like it when...

I resent...

I hate it when...

I'm fed up with...

I'm tired of...

I want...

2. Hurt and Sadness

I feel sad when...

I feel hurt because...

I feel awful because...

I feel disappointed because...

I want...

3. Fear and Insecurity

I feel afraid...

I'm afraid that...

I feel scared because...

I want...

4. Guilt and Responsibility

I'm sorry that...

I'm sorry for...

Please forgive me for...

I didn't mean to...

I wish...

5. Love, Forgiveness, Understanding and Desire

I love you because...

I love when...

Thank you for...

I understand that...

I forgive you for...

I want...

Remember:

if you want to feel better,

write a Love Letter!!

The Purpose of the Love Letter

The purpose of the Love Letter is to express and release all of the negative feelings preventing you from experiencing and sharing the love you feel deep inside. We call it a Love Letter not because it starts out "Dear Sweet Angel, I love you with all my heart...", but because *the purpose of the love letter is to resolve whatever emotions are in the way of the love flowing.* The structure of the love letter is based on those five levels of feeling mentioned earlier.

Why bother to sit down and write out all those feelings? The answer is simple:

Verbal Fighting Does Not Work

If I start out expressing anger with the intention of telling my partner my hurt, fear and guilt, finally working my way down to the love, I will never get that far — my partner will hear my anger, get angry herself, and interrupt me. Even it she agrees to just listen, looking at the expressions on her face and seeing her emotions will prevent me from smoothly working through my own feelings. By sitting down alone and writing out my feelings in a structured style (the Love Letter), I will give my emotions a chance to move and heal.

The second feature of the Love Letter technique is having someone read your letter back to you out loud. This serves several purposes:

1. You get to hear your own emotions expressed and externalized, thus making it easier for you to let go of them.

2. The person reading the letter will feel their own emotions as they read yours. When you move through to the love in your letter, they will feel themselves moving through to the love as well. If the reader was feeling separate, cold or emotionally shut down before reading your letter, they will certainly start to feel once they speak your words out loud.

How To Write A Love Letter

1. **Begin** — Sometimes the hardest part is deciding to write a Love Letter to a partner. Try not to be in the same room with them when you are writing. You do not need to feel loving to begin a love letter. No matter how you feel, if you want to feel better begin writing a love letter.

2. **Include all five levels of feeling** — Begin writing the letter at the first level of feeling (anger and blame) and gradually move through each level until you get to your positive feelings. Remember, the basic levels of emotion are:

    1. ANGER, BLAME and RESENTMENT
    2. HURT, SADNESS and DISAPPOINTMENT
    3. FEAR and INSECURITY
    4. GUILT, REGRET and "I'M SORRY"
    5. LOVE, FORGIVENESS, UNDERSTANDING and INTENTION

3. **Don't Edit Your Feelings** — The purpose of the Love Letter is to let all of your feelings out. A part of your mind might disagree with your feelings and some statements might not make any sense, but don't edit what you write. Your feelings will never make sense unless you clear out all of the incoherent, negative emotions.

DON'T TRY TO BE RATIONAL!! Allow the wounded, frightened, angry child inside to come out on paper. You can sound like a child throwing a temper tantrum. You can be a bitch or a jerk. You can bring out all the parts of yourself you are afraid to show. This is **not** the time to be nice, understanding or reasonable, especially in the first few sections of the letter; wait until you naturally get down to the love. Even if only one percent of you feels angry, express it as if all of you feels that way.

4. **Anger and Blame** — When you begin the letter with anger and blame, **don't be nice!** Indulge in that part of you that feels you are right and the other person is wrong. "You are so mean, you selfish jerk!" Let all that anger out. Don't intellectualize it. Here's an example of how NOT to do it: "I know your father never loved you and so you don't like to be

affectionate, but it disturbed me when you didn't kiss me goodnight." This person is analyzing their feelings instead of simply expressing them. For example: "I hate that you are never affectionate, you didn't even kiss me goodnight..."

5. Hurt and Sadness — After a while, you will start to notice some feelings of hurt and sadness coming up. You may even start to cry. That's because hurt and sadness are always underneath the anger and you will have released enough anger in your letter to start feeling the real hurt. When you notice this transition, go on to level two and write out your feelings of hurt and sadness: "I felt so hurt when you didn't kiss me goodnight. I feel devastated. How could you do this to me?"

6. Fear and Insecurity — After some time of expressing the hurt, you will begin to feel some fear or insecurity and you will go on to level three and write out those feelings: "I'm afraid you will never kiss me as much as I want. I'm afraid you are mad at me. I'm afraid you will leave me."

7. Guilt and "I'm Sorry" — After expressing your fears and getting more of a perspective on what you are really feeling, it is time to express the next level and to take responsibility for what you are writing about: "I'm sorry we don't always get along. I'm sorry I nagged you after work today and that's why you didn't want to kiss me...etc."

8. Love, Forgiveness, Understanding and Desire — After you have expressed all the other four levels of feeling, you will begin to feel the emotional connection with the person you are writing to and you will begin to become stronger again. You will naturally be in touch with your love, understanding and forgiveness. "I love you so much. You are a wonderful husband. I want to be more affectionate together, etc."

9. Don't Expect Yourself to be Aware of the Love When You Start the Letter — When you begin your Love Letter, you may just feel anger and resentment, maybe a little hurt and not much else. Just start expressing the anger and blame and you will see how quite naturally your emotions will progress into the next and then subsequent levels of feeling. **Don't wait to write the letter until you are in touch with the love!** That's just why you are writing it — to work through the emotions that are blocking you from feeling that love. Sometimes you may need to use some lead-in phrases and practice sentence completion to help you move through the different levels. We'll give you some more specific instructions later in this chapter.

10. **Repeating Levels** — You may find that you write out your anger, hurt and fear, and then all of a sudden you get angry again. That's fine. Jump back to the anger and remember to work your way back down through hurt and fear when you continue.

11. **Never Finish Your Love Letter Until You Have Gotten to the Love** — This is very important. If you stop writing before you get to the love, it is NOT a Love Letter. Getting up in the middle of your letter and giving up on writing it is giving up on making love work. Love is underneath, otherwise you wouldn't be so angry/hurt/afraid. So, just be patient, keep writing and it will come out.

12. **Balance the Sections of Your Love Letter** — Make sure your sections are balanced in length. Don't write three pages of anger, one page of hurt, two paragraphs of fear and guilt and one line of love at the end. That is **not** a love letter. There should always be a lot of love and appreciation at the end of the love letter. Every Love Letter should contain something from each of the five levels.

13. **Don't Defend Your Position or Just Explain Your Point of View** — *The purpose of the Love Letter is not to convey information alone, but to express emotion.*

So, for instance, you wouldn't write: "When you came home and told me what your boss said, I thought you meant that you would have to work late, so naturally I got upset. But I thought if I told you about it you would get angry, so I waited until after dinner."

That was an **explanation.** Instead, in a Love Letter you would say: "I hate when you work late. I hate when you don't come home to be with me. It makes me sad to see you work so hard. It hurts not to have you here. I'm afraid I don't see you enough. I'm afraid you will be mad at me for feeling this way."

See the difference?

14. **Write the Love Letter for Yourself, in Order to Resolve Your Own Emotions and Get Down to Your Own Love** — Don't write the Love Letter for the purpose of changing your partner, mother, etc. You will always feel better when you write a Love Letter so even if the other person refuses to write one also, go ahead and write yours.

What to do when You've Written a Love Letter to Your Partner

1. After you've finished writing your Love Letter, give it to your partner and ask him or her to read it back to you out loud, as if he's written it, as if he was the author of the letter. (Make sure to write clearly, or even type if you like).

2. The reader should try to read the letter back to the best of his ability, recreating the feelings of the writer. Sometimes, though, it is difficult to do a good job reading back the letter when you are reading your partner's negative thoughts about yourself. The reader's voice may become very monotone and controlling (especially if he is controlling his feelings while reading). *If your partner reads your letter back to you without much feeling, don't accuse them of doing it wrong!*

Ask them to read the letter over a few times out loud until their numbness wears off. As they continue to read the words, progressing down through all the different emotions and finally arriving at the love, their feelings will start to flow.

3. If your partner also wrote you a Love Letter, read it back to them after they have finished reading your letter. You may want to take turns reading the letters a few times in case you don't feel better after the first reading. Once you have read the other person's letter, you may also want to read your own letter out loud to your partner.

4. If your partner didn't write you a love letter, either because he refused or insisted he wasn't upset and you were the one who was, *don't be surprised if he gets upset reading your letter.* This means your letter was a success. Now your partner is in touch with his suppressed feelings and can write a Love Letter to you. When you express the truth, it creates the safety for your partner's feelings to come out, too.

5. If you are reading the letter and one line particularly upsets you or affects you, stop and read it over a few times. You probably feel upset because it brings out some strong feelings and re-reading will help you to release those emotions.

6. If you read the Love Letter with your partner and you still don't feel better, you can do the following:

   a. Write another letter — you may not have gotten out the deeper feelings.

   b. Read your letter out loud to your partner — this may help release the emotions.

   c. Re-read your partners letter and have them re-read yours.

   d. Put the Love Letters aside for an hour, and take some space from each other, planning to meet again to read them. **Do not communicate with your partner at all until then.**

Rules for Reading Love Letters

1. *Never stop reading a Love Letter until you have gotten to the end.* This is a sneaky way of hanging on to your partner's negative feelings about you without receiving their love and apology. Agree to read the whole letter, no matter what it says, all the way to the end.

2. *Do not make any comments while reading the letter,* such as: "How can you say this, you are worse than me!" or "You call me a jerk; you are the jerk." No comments are allowed. Just read the other person's feelings and feel your own.

Writing a Love Letter to Someone Other than an Intimate Partner

Writing Love Letters to people other than your partner (a parent, a child, a friend, sister, brother, boss, etc.) is a wonderful way to release and resolve negative emotions you have towards those people and feel more love and harmony in your relationships. However, if you write a Love Letter to your father or roommate or best friend, please follow this important guideline:

Do not, under any circumstances, give your Love Letter to the person you wrote it to, unless you have explained to them the format and purpose of the letter.

Exchanging Love Letters is appropriate for all relationships — family, friends, business and intimate. The Love Letter technique is **not** to be used as a chance to dump your negative feelings, but is an opportunity to share all your feelings back to the love and appreciation. It is good to tone down the anger section in the beginning. If you send a letter to your mother and it reads: "You are such a jerk, mom. You have ruined my whole life," she may go into shock! **Don't expect the people in your life to share Love Letters with you without a clear understanding of the principles.** In some cases, it may not be appropriate to a share a Love Letter. However, you can write those letters and then have a friend read them.

1. If you've written a Love Letter to a person you are not close to or to someone who is unable to respond, ask someone close to you to read it back to you out loud. This will have a wonderful effect on both of you. You may want to send a Love Letter without the anger section. Or, if you write a Love Letter to your three year old son, ask your husband to read it back to you.

2. If you've written the letter to someone who doesn't understand the Love Letter technique, then after you've written the letter and have resolved your feelings, you can communicate the complete truth to that person either verbally, on the phone or in a letter. For example:

"You know, Mom, last week I was **angry** at you for calling me up and complaining so much about your health. It **hurts** me to hear you sound sick and I get **afraid** that your illness will get worse. I feel helpless because I can't do anything to help you and I'm **sorry** I get so impatient sometimes. I **love** you and want you to take better care of yourself and get well!" Notice how this communication contained all five levels of feeling. You will be able to communicate this effortlessly and without emotional charge after having written out all of the more intense feelings in a complete Love Letter and having had someone read it back to you.

3. Once you become comfortable with Love Letters and you share this book with family members, you can surely use the Love Letter technique together. Just be sure that everyone understands the rules on how to write correct Love Letters and the philosophy behind them contained in this section of the book. We have had wonderful success using Love Letters with parents and children, brothers and sisters, etc.

167

What To Do When Your Partner Won't Read Your Love Letter or Write One

Sometimes you (or your partner) will decide to write a Love Letter to resolve a conflict and the other person will refuse to do the technique. What should you do?

1. Don't use their refusal as an excuse to hang on to your own negative feelings — go write that Love Letter anyway. You are doing it for yourself. You win by letting go of all those emotions in the way of your love.

2. When you are finished with your letter, present your partner with it and ask them to read it.

3. If your partner refuses to read the letter, **do not under any circumstances continue to communicate with him until he has read it.** If you do, you are sure to get into a fight instantaneously, unless you totally suppress your feelings, which is just as bad. Simply tell the other person: "I felt much better writing this letter. I'd like you to read it so we can make up. Until you do, I don't want to communicate with you because I know we will start fighting. I'll check back with you in a while." Then go about your business and come back in an hour or whatever time you feel is appropriate. If he still refuses to read the letter, leave and try again later. After awhile, your partner will get curious as to what is in the letter and will agree to read it. If he doesn't, you need to seriously reevaluate the relationship you are in and decide if it works for you to be with a partner who won't cooperate and participate in healing conflicts.

What To Do When You Are Finished Reading Your Letters

Never throw away your Love Letters. We suggest you keep them all in one place, in a drawer or notebook. Then, if you are in a hurry one day, pick out an old one and give it to your partner to read to you. You will be surprised to find that the majority of your Love Letters are about the same topics. Most couples fight about the same things over and over again and have their ten basic Love Letter topics.

Topic #1: Why don't you do more work? Topic #2: Why are you so critical of me? Topic #3: I hate it when you shut down — and so on. In a pinch, pull out a Love Letter on the same topic you are fighting about and use it, first by reading it out loud yourself and then having your partner read it back to you. Don't rely on this method, however, since it is always best to write a "fresh" Love Letter.

The other value of saving Love Letters is that you will be able to monitor your growth and see how much progress you are making in making love work in your life. Re-read your old Love Letters when you are not upset, to get a new perspective on how small your emotional mountains really look when you are feeling loved and loving. When you are emotionally upset, things are easily blown out of proportion. Re-reading Love Letters will give your subconscious mind valuable feedback and will be a good reference point for balancing future emotional reactions.

Remember: as old conflicts heal and old issues are taken care of, new conflicts will come up and new issues will emerge until all of your repressed feelings get healed. Every conflict, upset or crisis becomes an opportunity to draw on deeper levels of your loving potential when you use the Love Letter Technique as a map to explore your feelings.

What To Do In An Emotional Emergency

Have you ever started a fight with your partner just as you were about to enter a restaurant?

Have you ever planned a big party and just before the guests arrived, you started arguing with your husband or wife?

What can you do when you need to write a Love Letter but only have 5 minutes?

Write A Mini Love Letter!!

Take out a piece of paper, napkin, an envelope, anything will do, and write just one sentence on each of the five levels of feeling. For example: Maxine feels Sean is not appreciating how she looks and they are just about to walk into a restaurant and meet some friends:

Dear Sean:
1) I'm so angry at you for acting like such a jerk and not telling me I look beautiful.
2) It really hurts me when you don't pay attention to me or think I'm special.
3) I'm afraid you aren't proud of me and don't care like you used to.
4) I'm sorry I overreact sometimes and shut down to you.
5) I love you so much and want to have a wonderful time tonight. Let's make up.

Love,
Maxine

Even though Maxine doesn't have time to express more of the anger and hurt, she will now be more in touch with her complete feelings and so will Sean. Later, when they have more time, they can write longer versions of the Love Letter to really resolve the issue.

Hints To Make Writing Your First Few Love Letters Easier

1. If you and a partner want to use the Love Letter Technique but are a little nervous about really letting each other have it in the Love Letter or if you want to feel more confident with the results of using the technique, here's what we suggest: each of you write a Love Letter to someone in your life other than your partner (i.e., to your mother, your father, your boss, etc.) Then exchange Love Letters and read your partner's back to them. When you see how good you feel reading and writing Love Letters and how much more loving you feel towards the person you wrote the Love Letter to, even though they aren't present, you will begin to trust the Love Letter process. Now you can try writing them to each other with a little more certainty that they do work.

2. Your first few Love Letters may be quite long and it may take you some time to get through the anger down to the other emotions, especially if your relationship has had a lot of repressed feelings. We suggest you don't try to include every emotion you've ever had about your partner in one letter. If your love letters take up too much time, then try dealing with specific issues, rather than trying to handle sex, money, power, communication and compatibility all in one letter.

Helpful Tips For Writing Love Letters

After years of writing love letters and guiding others through their feelings, I have developed various techniques for allowing each level of feeling to be fully expressed. When the emotional tension at each level is released through writing, you can effortlessly slide into the next level. Let's look at each level separately.

Level One — Anger and Blame

If you are emotionally upset in any way or if you are emotionally numb, you are feeling some anger inside. You may not be aware of that anger, because it is easy to suppress. It is absolutely essential to begin each Love Letter by expressing that anger. Without expressing and releasing anger, you can never get to the deeper level of love which is inside of you.

If you are stuck, you may want to use any of these lead-in phrases to help you express and release your anger:

"I hate it when..."

"I don't like it when..."

"If I weren't a nice person, I'd be angry that..."

"I get angry when..."

"I'm fed up with..."

Here is an example of using the lead in phrase: "I get angry when..."

"I get angry when you don't compliment me."

"I get angry when you complain all day."

"I get angry when you don't listen to me."

Simply repeat the lead-in phrase and then complete the sentence with whatever feeling comes up.

The anger section of the Love Letter is a time to let out all of your criticism and blame without trying to be reasonable or responsible. I like to think of it as having a temper tantrum on paper. This is the time to let that child inside of you come out. It is perfectly alright to use all sorts of psychological no-no's like:

You always do that."

You are never on time."

You should grow up."

Feel free to complain all that you want. Let the judgemental side of you completely express itself.

It's important to allow yourself to generalize and even indulge in name calling, but give yourself a chance to be specific too. For example, instead of just saying: "I hate when you are mean to me", try saying: "I hate when you are mean to me. How could you just leave me standing at the mall waiting for two hours?" Writing: "I hate you, I hate you" over and over is too general. It must become more specific for there to be a release. Some people yell and scream generalities and think they are releasing emotional tension, when the results they achieve are due more to repression through exhaustion.

It is also valuable to periodically interject your expectations and intentions throughout each level. "I want" is the most powerful intention phrase. Let's see how it would fit in with Level One — Anger and Blame:

"**I hate you when** you treat me like I am ruining your life. **I hate when** you say you don't care. **I hate when** you lose control and yell at me. **I hate** when you ignore me. **I want you** to show me you care. **I want you** to think I'm wonderful. **I hate your** weakness. **I want you** to take responsibility for our problems too."

Here are some more helpful lead in phrases:

"**It makes me sick when**..."

"**I'm so tired of listening** to your complaints..."

"**You are such a jerk**..."

"**You act like** an idiot..."

"**How do you think I feel when**..."

"**How can you**..."

When you have completed the Anger section, move on to Hurt and Sadness.

Level Two — Hurt and Sadness

Some phrases to help you express this second level of emotion are:

"I feel sad when..."

"I feel sad because..."

"It hurts when..."

"The reason I feel hurt is..."

"I feel disappointed that..."

"It makes me sad to think..."

173

"It makes me sad to see you..."

Just as in Level One, it is valuable to use intention phrases such as:

"I want..."

"I need..."

For example, a woman might have these feelings towards her partner:

"**It hurts when** you don't pull me to you and want to kiss and hug me. **It hurts when you** aren't attracted to me. **I feel sad that** you don't have a good time with me. **I want you** to compliment me. **It made me feel awful** that you didn't notice my new dress. **I want you** to be proud of me."

When you have completed level two, move on to expressing your fears.

Level Three — Fear and Insecurity

"**I'm afraid that** you don't like me..."

"**I'm afraid you** will hurt me again..."

"**I'm afraid you** don't care anymore."

"**I'm afraid I** won't be able to make you happy."

"**I'm afraid you** can't forgive me..."

"**I'm afraid you** won't like this letter..."

As before, it is helpful to intersperse intention phrases into this section:

"I want..." "I need..." "I wish..." For example:

"**I'm afraid** we'll never get along. **I'm afraid** our marriage will get worse. **I'm afraid** you'll never change. **I'm afraid** I will never be good enough for you. **I'm afraid** you'll hurt me. **I want you** to appreciate me. **I want you** to accept me. **I need** to feel safe with you. **I wish you** could accept me just the way I am."

When you are finished with this level, go on to the next level: Guilt and Responsibility.

Level Four — Guilt and Responsibility

Most people believe that to feel guilty or sorry, they must be wrong or solely responsible. This notion prevents us from feeling our natural feelings of guilt. You don't have to have caused hurt or injury to another to feel sorry. If my mother is sick, I feel sorry. If I accidently hurt someone, I feel sorry even though I am innocent. In Level Four of the

174

Love Letter, you have an opportunity to express and release your feelings of guilt and responsiblity:

"**I'm sorry** I hurt you..."

"**I'm sorry** I can't make you happy..."

"**I'm sorry** I am mean sometimes..."

"**I'm sorry** we had an argument..."

"**I'm sorry** I get so frustrated and angry..."

"**I'm sorry** I criticized you in front of those people..."

"**I'm sorry** I do such stupid things..."

"**Please forgive me for** pushing you away..."

"**I feel bad because** I embarassed you..."

You can also put in those intentional phrases such as: "I want..." and "I wish..."

An example of blending the guilt and the intentions is:

"**I'm sorry** we are fighting again. **I'm sorry** I got so angry. **I'm sorry** I waited so long before writing this letter. **I'm sorry** I don't make you happy. **I'm sorry** we hurt each other. **I want** to have a wonderful vacation with you. **I want** to make up and be loving. **I want** to always write you Love Letters rather than yell and fight. **I'm sorry** I lose my temper. **I want** to accept you and support you. **I want you** to be happy. **I didn't mean to** ruin our trip. **I wanted** to have a wonderful time. **Please forgive me** for throwing a tantrum. **I should** have written a Love Letter first. **I'm so sorry** I hurt you."

Remember, when you are expressing your guilt, don't defend yourself. The purpose of the Love Letter is not to be right or wrong. It is to share your honest feelings. **You don't have to be wrong to feel guilty or sorry.** Saying you are sorry gives your partner an opportunity to love and forgive you.

Having completed the guilt section, it becomes very easy and genuine to express feelings of love, forgiveness, understanding and intention.

Level Five — Love, Forgiveness, Understanding and Intention

When you have fully expressed and released the emotions from the first four levels, the natural outcome is a feeling of love and acceptance. Acceptance doesn't mean you are totally in agreement with another's behavior — just that you are willing to love again. We define the word forgive as the willingness to give as before: for-give. I can love you even

175

Love Letter Technique

though I don't agree with what you did. Once you have let go of the anger, hurt, fear and guilt, you are ready to feel and fully express the love.

"**I love** being with you."
"**I love you because** you are so sensitive."
"**I think you are** the most wonderful wife in the world."
"**You give me** so much confidence in myself."
"**I love when** you kiss me."
"**I love** the way you play with me."
"**I love** how you dress up for me."
"**I am so grateful that** you want to be with me."
"**I need you to** hold me."
"**I support you** in telling me the truth."
"**I forgive you for** being so critical."
"**I understand that** you felt threatened."
"**Thank you for** being so loving."

Intention phrases should definitely be used in the love section. "I want...", "I need...", "I will...", "I promise to...", "I know..." For example:

"**I love you** so much. **I need you** to love me. **I want you** to always love me. **I will try to** be more accepting. **I love** being with you. **You are** so much fun. **I think you** are so talented. **I love when** you open up to me. **I will try** to stay open to you. **I think** we are wonderful together. **I know you** don't want to hurt me. **I forgive you** for being mean to me sometimes. **You can** be so sweet. **I love you** and **I want you** to love me. Let's make up."

It may happen that when you get down to the guilt and the love, you start feeling angry all over again. That means there is still some suppressed anger that you didn't express in the beginning. Just start writing it out and gradually you will come back to the love. If you do feel anger or hurt again after you've finished those sections, write out those feelings and go through the four levels again, even one sentence on each until you get back to the love.

Allow yourself to really let go in the love section — don't be too intellectual. Express your feelings in the superlative: "You are the best husband in the world." Let your partner know why you love them. No one gets tired of hearing how much they are loved. Telling your partner (mother, daughter, etc.) you love them is never redundant. Remember, you are not merely conveying information, you are allowing the feelings to flow. Expressing them through words helps them to flow out of you more freely. When love isn't continuously expressed, it gradually stops flowing. And when love stops flowing, you stop feeling it.

If you are writing a Love Letter to someone with whom you are not passionately in love, of course your love section will be different. Here are some lead-in phrases for those kinds of Love Letters:

"**I really appreciate you for** being such a wonderful friend..."
"**Thank you** for helping me..."
"**I like it when** you give me feedback."
"**I love your** sense of humor."
"**I support you in** getting what you want."
"**I understand** you are doing your best."
"**You really are** a wonderful boss."
"**I'm so grateful that** you are my brother."
"**I think you are** a wonderful teacher."

Don't try to force or fake your love in this section. There are some people whom you will never like because you don't have much in common. But you can write a Love Letter to that person if you are really angry and in the love section, try to understand their loving intention and forgive them. Try to see if there is anything you can relate to about them. You can always find at least some good will towards a person. And remember, what you cannot forgive in others, you may end up repeating in order to understand their behavior.

The Love Section of the Love Letter is a chance for you to rediscover the tremendous amount of love and appreciation you have inside of you. It works because you took the time to express all of the other emotional layers which cover up the love: the anger, hurt, fear and guilt. Working with this powerful technique will give you confidence and the certainty that underneath all negative emotions love is always waiting to be expressed and experienced and that all it takes is your telling the complete truth about all of your feelings.

Sample Love Letters

I wanted to include some sample Love Letters to give you an idea of what a real Love Letter sounds like. These are actual letters I've collected from our clients and people attending our seminars.

Tim and Jane

(Tim and Jane were having a fight about doing work around the house. These are their Love Letters to each other. They are relatively short ones.)

Dear Tim:

You stupid jerk. What's the matter with you? I am sick of acting like a nag to get you out of bed in the morning. I hate your laziness. Why can't you get out of bed, you lazy bum? You never get anything done. There's so much to do and you just sleep. Well, it makes me sick. And then you get mad at me for trying to get you out of bed. It makes me so furious. I hate when you make me feel like a nag.

It hurts me when you get mad at me and I'm only trying to help. It hurts me when you think I'm a nag. It hurts me to see you so tired because I want you to feel good. It hurts me that we fight like this. I feel sad that we have different time schedules and that you need more sleep. I feel sad that we hurt each other.

I'm afraid you will make me into a perpetual nag. I'm afraid you could stop loving me because of it. I'm afraid we will take forever to fix up the house because you sleep so much. I'm afraid I won't see enough of you these next few years because of school and work and sleep. I'm afraid you won't be able to give me help with the baby because you will be so tired.

I'm sorry for nagging you. I'm sorry you are so tired. I'm sorry for getting you out of bed. I think I do it just because I miss you and want to be with you. I'm sorry that you have to work so hard and get so tired. I'm sorry I don't help more.

Tim, I really love you so much. You are a wonderful husband and we share so much together. I am so lucky to be sharing my life with you. I feel such joy being with you every day. I know you really love me and care for me. You are a wonderful person and I am so proud of you. I love all the work you've done around the house. I forgive you for getting so tired; I get tired too. I am so happy loving you. Thank you for being so good to me.

I love you, Jane

Dear Jane:

What is the matter with you? Can't you lay off? Nag, nag, nag! If you think you're so great, why don't you fix up the kitchen? I hate you when you treat me like this. I don't see you drilling any damned holes or putting up shelves. I hate your complaining. I want you to appreciate the work I'm doing for you, not put me down all the time. I hate it.

It hurts so much to feel I'm not perfect and make mistakes. It hurts me that you don't feel I am a good enough husband for you. It hurts when you say I'm lazy. I feel sad that I don't know more about fixing up the house and doing it right. It hurts when I make a mistake and you point it out to me.

I'm afraid that I am going to go through my entire life goofing up every step of the way. I am afraid I am working too hard. I am afraid you will look at me as some sort of clumsy, goofy clown. I'm afraid I won't have enough time to do everything I want to do. I want to have more time to play together, not just to work or fix up the house.

I'm sorry, because the truth is I am really mad at myself to have taken out my frustration on you. I am sorry I lost my temper. I am sorry I yelled at you. I'm sorry I am so lazy sometimes. I'm sorry I don't know more about fixing up the house. I feel so ashamed of myself when I lose my temper.

Jane, I really, really love you. I can't say it enough. I just hope you see my love for you radiating from my face and flowing from my heart. You are a terrific wife and I love living with you. I can't imagine another woman being more perfect for me. I appreciate your love so much; I need it so much. I want you to be proud of me. I want our house to be beautiful. I want our life to be wonderful. I want to be a great husband for you. I love you and want to make you happy.

Love, Tim

Jo Anne's Love Letter To Her Boyfriend

Dear Frank,

You are such a self-centered jerk. I hate you for the way you acted at that party. How dare you leave me alone while you went and talked to that woman for 20 minutes? I've never been so angry in my life. You make me sick. You are just like every man I've met, all you care about is your big ego and your sex life. Well, I have had it. I hated seeing you flirt with that little bitch. I hated feeling I would intrude if I came up. I hate you for making me feel so bad and ruining my night. And, I am so angry at you for acting like it was no big deal when I complained, and making me feel I was overreacting. I wanted to be with you at that party and you ruined everything.

I feel so hurt by what you did. My heart is breaking. I feel so sad thinking you may be getting tired of me. I felt awful watching you laughing and joking with her, while I sat alone. It hurts so much when you push me away. It hurts when you hide from our love. It hurts me when you think I'm not good enough for you. I felt so sad tonight, feeling us so distant from each other. I want to feel close all the time. It hurts me when you give so much attention to the other women and ignore me. Please understand how I feel. I need you to make me feel special.

I'm afraid that you will leave me. I'm afraid you aren't in love with me anymore. I'm afraid you find other women more attractive than me. I'm afraid I will be jealous and you will get angry with me. I'm afraid I'm not good enough for you. I'm afraid I can't handle the competition. I'm afraid this issue will always come between us. I'm afraid of being alone.

I'm sorry I attacked you when we got home. I'm sorry I don't trust you more. I'm sorry I shut down to you and was so cold during our love making afterwards. I'm sorry we fight. I'm sorry I get so jealous. I know you love me and were just having a great conversation. I'm sorry I clam up at parties sometimes. I guess I am just insecure about being around people.

I want to trust you more. I want us to be so happy. I want you to include me when you are having fun. I want to love you and make you proud of me. I want to learn not to feel threatened when we aren't together all the time.

Frank, I love you so much. This is the most wonderful relationship I have ever had. You are so supportive of me and I think you are a terrific man. Being with you makes me so happy. Your kindness and sensitivity is precious to me.

I love living together with you. I love the way you listen to me and really care about what I feel. Thank you for wanting to use Love Letters to clear up our fights. Thank you for being understanding with me about my insecurities. Thank you for making me feel like a beautiful women. I want to feel that way more. I need you so much in my life. I want to grow together and love each other more every day.

Love, Jo Anne

Bonnie's Letter To Her Father

NOTE: Bonnie didn't give this to her father. She wrote it and had someone else read it back to her. She then toned down the anger section and gave it to her father to read back to her.

Dear Dad:

What a jerk you are. You have never liked me. You have never supported me. You never understood me. I hate you for being so cold to me all these years. I hate you for being so mean and unloving. You are the most self-centered person in the world. You are such an creep — all you do is drink and complain. I hate you for never being there for Mom. I hate you for never liking her or supporting her. I hated watching you mistreat her all those years. You make me sick. I'm ashamed of you. I hate your disgusting drinking. I hate your weakness. I hate you because you were never really a father.

It hurts me that you never cared for me. It hurts me that you were never really loving to me. It hurts that you never played with me. I never had a father. I never even really knew you, and that makes me so sad. It hurts to think of how much we missed. It hurts me to know you are hurting and killing yourself with alcohol. It hurts me to feel so angry towards you. I want to feel close to you, not angry. I want to be proud of you. It hurts me to feel so ashamed of you.

181

I'm afraid that you really don't like me. I'm afraid no one has ever wanted me. I'm afraid we will never be closer. I'm afraid I can never forgive you. I want to forgive you. I want to love and accept you.

I'm sorry I don't always love you. I'm sorry I don't call you more. I'm sorry that I have pushed you out of my life. I'm sorry I sometimes wish I had a different father. I'm sorry you are so miserable. I'm sorry I can't help you. I'm sorry your life has been so hard. I'm sorry I can't make you happy. I want you to be happy. I want you to stop drinking.

I want you to know how much I do love you underneath. I want to be closer with you. Thank you for all the things you've done for me. I know you have tried. I know it has been hard on you too. I love those funny parts of you. I love the times we are close. Your love means so much to me. I want us to love each other and be friends. I want you to be happy. You are so important to me.

Love, Bonnie

Children's Love Letters

Dad:

You make me furious. I get so angry when you yell at Mom. I hate when you don't want to come and visit me. I feel sad that you don't act proud of what I want to be when I grow up. I feel sad that you don't live here anymore. I'm afraid you won't ever really love me. I'm afraid you won't be proud of me. I'm sorry that you smoke. I love you a lot!

Love, Pollyanna   Age 10

Dear Mom:

I hate when you talk about me to your friends. It embarrasses me. I feel sad that you have to embarrass me like that. I'm afraid one time I will tell you something private and you'll tell someone. I'm sorry I don't want you to talk about me. I love you very much. Please ask me before you talk about me.

Love, Matt   Age 13

Dear Mom,

I'm angry because you hit me. I'm sad when you yell at me. I'm afraid when you yell at me and get angry. I'm sorry I didn't listen to you. I love you because you are very special.

Love, Ari   Age 9

Writing A Love Letter to Yourself

A wonderful way to motivate yourself is to write a Love Letter to yourself. Rather than moping around, feeling down on yourself, being self-critical or depressed, sit down and write a Love Letter to you, starting with the anger and moving down to the love. This way you don't stay stuck in the negative feelings which can immobilize you and thus make things even worse.

Dear Mary,

You really piss me off. I hate when you give everybody else so much power. I hate when you still think that you can't ask for help; that you don't deserve it; that what's going on for you is not important enough. What's wrong with you? Do you think you always have to have a major trauma going on before you deserve attention?

It makes me very sad that you don't love yourself enough yet to know you deserve attention and love just for being yourself. It hurts to not ask. It hurts to be afraid to ask. It's sad to see you be such a little helpless child.

I'm afraid you'll never see how you deserve attention and love. I'm afraid you'll always feel guilty for asking for help. I'm afraid you'll have to create major drama in order to ask for help and you'll still feel guilty about it.

I'm sorry you don't love yourself more easily. I'm sorry you still feel like the small little girl who doesn't deserve attention.

You really do deserve love and attention. I want you to ask for what you want and express your feelings about how you feel. I want you to love yourself enough to not feel guilty when you get attention and special treatment. You are totally deserving of that treatment and you deserve love. You are sweet and generous and help so many people and you need and deserve your time too. I want you to ask for what you want and need, and feel OK about it. I love you. You are deserving and loving.

Love, Mary

Chapter 9

Love Is Not Enough

Falling in love is an irresistible experience. When you first fall in love, everything seems so easy and it's hard to imagine that you won't feel that way forever.

But love is not enough to keep a relationship going. Cupid's arrows may bring you a wonderful evening, or week, or month with your lover, but you need a lot more than love to make your relationship work for a lifetime.

Cupid's arrows may bring you a loving evening but they are not enough to keep a relationship going.

Love and compatibility must go hand in hand for a relationship to last.

If two people are not compatible with each other, their relationship is destined to die. Love and compatibility must go hand in hand for a relationship to work and keep on working. In counseling couples, I have found that ten to twenty percent of marriages were incompatible to start with. The couple never felt out their similarities and differences long enough to decide whether or not they could live together in peace and harmony.

Feeling mutual need in a relationship creates passion and excitement.

When you and your partner are growing in the same direction and share a common vision for yourself and the relationship, you will naturally complement each other. You will need each other to help you in your individual growth and to help make the whole complete. Feeling mutual need in a relationship creates passion and excitement. The first heat of passionate love is enticing, but a relationship must be based on mutual need if it is going to survive.

Love is not enough. If two people are not going in the same direction and growing together, then their love will be torn.

Compatibility means that you and your partner have similar dreams and goals and that you agree on the ways in which you want to achieve those goals, both separately and together. It means that the way you enjoy living and being is very similar to the way in which your partner enjoys living and being. Every relationship should serve a purpose and have a direction. If two people are not going in the same direction and growing together, their love will be torn apart.

Compatibility doesn't mean that you and your partner are exactly alike. Differences create attraction and if both people in a relationship were identical, the relationship would soon become boring. If those differences are too great, however, they produce conflict and tension rather than just stimulation and balance.

If your partner was exactly like you, it would get very boring. Differences create attraction.

Love by itself is not enough. Love, Compatibility, and Know-how are the essential ingredients for making relationships work.

Make a list of what you want in a relationship and in a partner, and ask your partner to do the same. Then compare lists and see if your goals are or can be compatible. If you and your partner are compatible, for the most part you are off to a good start.

But even if you have love and compatibility, your relationship may not work unless you have one additional ingredient — the tools and techniques for resolving conflicts and tension on a daily basis. By working with the techniques in the previous section, you can avoid building up the emotional tension in your relationship and killing the love.

It's also important to plan time for intimacy in your relationship just as you would plan to go to work or to exercise.   I suggest at least three separate times a week for what I call "Planned Intimacy." Planned Intimacy is a time for sharing feelings, talking, loving (with no specific sexual expectations). It is a time for just you and your partner, with no interruptions. By planning time for your relationship, you are making sure to keep it healthy and growing.

Planning time for intimacy is just as important as scheduling time for work and play.

People keep their wants and feelings secret and then expect their partner to do exactly what they want.

Chapter 10
Asking For What You Want

Some people resent having to ask for what they want in a relationship. They feel: "If my partner really loves me, he will know what to do." Don't expect your partner to know what's inside of you or to read your mind. Tell him or her what you want, and don't forget to ask what they want from you too. If you aren't getting what you want, start letting your partner know in advance and not just after the letdown. Keeping what you want a secret is a sure way to build up feelings of resentment and hurt between you and your partner.

You and your partner can't always have everything you want in your relationship, but if you are compatible, you can work it out so that both of you can be satisfied. Ask for what you want and be willing to negotiate so that you both get your needs met. In this way, you and your partner both win and no one loses.

If you are not getting what you want, start letting your partner know in advance and not just after the let down.

In a relationship, ask for what you want and be willing to negotiate so that both of you can be satisfied.

***You don't have to wait for compliments or fish for them.
If you are not getting the love you want then ask for it.***

At times you may feel that your partner doesn't appreciate you. Some people decide that if they are not getting enough love, they will leave rather than ask for it. They think to themselves: "I don't want to beg for love." Asking for what you want is not begging. If you aren't getting the love and appreciation you want, it's your responsibility to ask for it. Assume that your partner wants to support you and only needs some guidance from you. You don't have to wait for compliments or fish for them. You deserve to be appreciated.

Try spending a few moments at the end of each day appreciating each other for all you have done. Take turns saying: "Something I appreciate about you is..." Let your partner know some of the things you feel you should be appreciated for by saying: "Something you should appreciate me for is..."

Remember, appreciation is a two-way street. If you are sitting around waiting for your partner (or your friends) to appreciate you, stop and ask yourself if you have been expressing your appreciation for him or her. Appreciation is contagious. The more you express your gratitude for others, the safer they will feel in expressing their gratitude for you. Tell your partner *why* you love him or her, not just *that* you love him. No one ever gets tired of hearing all the reasons they are loved. Be specific — conditional love gives meaning and significance to love and personalizes it.

Tell your partner why *you love her, not just* that *you love her. Conditional love gives meaning and significance to love and personalizes it.*

Many people confuse submission with love. A sure-fire way to kill the love in a relationship is to sacrifice your wants.

Many people confuse submission with love: "If she loves me, she will do what I want," or "I will do it because I love you, even though I really don't want to do it." A sure-fire way to kill the love in a relationship is to sacrifice your wants and needs in order to be loved by someone else. When you stop caring about yourself and your needs, there are no longer two people in the relationship. It's hard to be interested in nobody.

To love another doesn't mean you make them more important than yourself. There is nothing more boring than being in a relationship with someone who feels they have no self-worth. You are mistaken if you think that you will impress your partner by treating him as if he is better than you. If you care more about your partner than yourself, one day you will find that your partner starts caring only about himself too.

To love another doesn't mean you make them more important than yourself.

***For love to last there must be equal caring — first about
yourself and then your partner.***

For love to last, there must be equal caring, first about yourself and
then about your partner. Caring about yourself and your needs gives
your partner an opportunity to love and support you.

Some people sacrifice in their relationships by taking upon themselves all the chores and duties without letting their partner know how hard they are working, and then secretly they resent their plight. If you fall into this category, try scheduling family business meetings where you sit down and make lists of all the duties and jobs that must be done. Point out how much you usually do, and let everyone present pick out the things they enjoy doing most, and split the other duties. If there is a job no one likes doing, take turns doing it or hire someone else to do it. In this way, nothing gets taken for granted and you will find that you are being appreciated more.

When you share your list of duties, nothing gets taken for granted and you will find that you are appreciated much more.

For most nice people, "hate" is a dirty word. Unexpressed hate will lead to an inability to feel love.

Chapter 11

Love Doesn't Mean Being Nice All The Time

To love a person doesn't mean you will always agree with them or even feel good about them. It doesn't mean you will like all of the things they do or don't do. Nobody is perfect. Whenever you like a person, there will always be some things you dislike too. And if you really love someone, it inevitably happens that sometimes you not only dislike what they do, but that you hate it.

For most people, "hate" is a dirty word. It's thought to be a taboo to feel hate towards your partner. That's only allowed during the divorce proceedings!

Hate is really just a symptom of obstructed love. When you love someone and they do something that is hard for you to love and accept, the natural reaction is to hate that behavior. You want to change that person, so you can love them again.

All suppressed resentment culminates in hate. If you don't give yourself permission to express your hate in appropriate ways, it gets repressed, and along with it, you repress your ability to love fully.

When you can't share and express your negative feelings, they build up and get blown out of proportion. Or you may work very hard at repressing them and think they are forgotten. They may be forgotten but they still have an effect — you are cursed to emotionally overreact in your relationships.

When you can't share, express and resolve your negative feelings, they build up and get blown up out of proportion.

Suppressed anger is contagious; it gets passed from one person to another.

It is not very difficult to resolve negative feelings. The only thing you need to do is tell the **complete** truth about them. Many people attempt to do this and find it doesn't work, because when they become angry, their partner just becomes angry back. Getting angry back and forth makes it even more difficult for you to let go of the negative feelings and find the love and forgiveness.

The solution is simple, but powerful. Whenever you begin to notice your resentment, sit down and write a Love Letter to your partner, following the instructions in Chapter 8. Express all your anger and resentment, moving down through your hurt, fear, and guilt, and miraculously a new rush of love will bubble up and you will be able to genuinely forgive your partner and be in love again.

To forgive a person doesn't mean that you agree with their behavior. To forgive is to resolve your emotional resistance so that your love can flow as freely as it did before. To forgive is to **give** your love as **before** (for-give).

Suppressed anger is contagious, and most families today are suffering from an epidemic of it. Unexpressed anger usually gets acted out through our behavior. You may end up taking out your frustration

Getting angry back and forth doesn't work, but generally makes things worse.

on some innocent bystander, or your wife and children, and they pass it along. Trying to be nice and kind by suppressing your negative feelings only allows them to build up until you either explode irrationally or you become so repressed that you have numbed your ability to feel positive emotions.

To forgive does not imply that you agree with another's behavior.

To forgive is to give *your love as* before — *for-give.*

When you express all of your negative emotions, you will naturally arrive at a feeling of forgiveness. Forgiveness means an emotional acceptance of what happened. Now you can work towards preventing its repetition. It is a willingness to let go of what happened and find the love again — not forgetting about it, but expressing the resentment so that the emotional tension is dissolved, and then expressing your willingness to for-give.

The process of releasing your negative feelings and coming to a genuine state of love and forgiveness is essential for your personal growth. When you stop loving, it is you who suffers the most. When you hold on to anger and resentment, it is you who misses out on the love. When you are willing to work through your negative emotions back down to your willingness to love, you are the one who is the winner.

When you stop loving, it is you who suffers.

By giving yourself permission to feel and heal your hate and negative emotions, the obstructed love inside can flow again. Expressing the negative feelings that come up in a relationship is not a sign of weakness or failure — on the contrary, it is a sign of strength that you are committed to resolving whatever negative emotions get in the way of your feeling in love all the time.

Before you leave a relationship give your partner a chance to work on the relationship.

Chapter 12

Breaking Up With Love

Many times when we want to leave a person, we start gathering evidence to justify saying goodbye. We start keeping a mental list of all of your partner's "crimes", and then one day we spring it on them: "Here is the evidence. You are bad. I have been abused and so I have a reason to leave."

Before ending a relationship, it is important to resolve the build-up of negative emotions towards your partner and to feel the love and gratitude again. When the love in a relationship gets repressed due to a continued lack of communication, you are bound to feel less love for your partner. But just as you cannot tell if you are right for each other without love, so you cannot tell if you are wrong for each other without feeling the love and seeing the reasons why you got together in the first place.

You do not have to stop loving your partner to leave them. If you are honest with yourself and have resolved your resentments towards your partner, you will always feel love towards them.

If you have thoughts about leaving your partner, give them advance warning. Offer them a chance to work on the relationship with you. Tell your partner what you want and what you are not getting, and give them a bottom line.

Many times, in order to end a relationship, we start gathering evidence to justify saying: "Goodbye, I don't love you any more."

207

***When you leave a partner without resolving your feelings,
you carry those feelings into your next relationship.***

Work together on expressing and releasing all of your suppressed
feelings of anger, hurt, fear and guilt. By telling the complete truth
about your emotions, you can get back in touch with your love again.
That doesn't mean you have to stay — it means if you still want to leave,
you can leave in friendship and not in animosity.

You can still love a person and say "no" simply because deep inside
your heart you know he is not right for you. Or you may be surprised to
find that once you've resolved some of your negative feelings, you start
to feel hope again, and a renewed desire to try to make it work. The
majority of couples who break up still have tremendous potential for a
successful relationship, but the love is buried under years of repressed
anger and hurt that needs to be healed.

To leave a partner while you still have unresolved feelings of hurt and anger can be very dangerous (unless your partner is really awful, of course). Generally what happens is that you carry all of those stuffed feelings right into your next relationship. Soon they start affecting your new relationship, and very quickly you find yourself in the same mess you just left.

All of the relationships you've been in that didn't work are golden opportunities for you to learn from. It's important to learn from the mistakes of the past in order to prevent them from happening again. Rather than blaming your previous partners for being wrong, take a look at what you both did wrong in the relationship so you can avoid repeating those same mistakes in your next relationship.

We must learn from the mistakes of the past to prevent them from happening again.

Let your commitment to the truth be a turning point in your life.

Chapter 13

The Gift Of Love

Solving the mystery of love can be the most exciting adventure of your life. It takes a willingness to always stay in touch with your feelings and to tell the complete truth about them to yourself and others. Let your commitment to the truth be a turning point in your life.

The more you tell the truth in your life, the more you will learn to trust your feelings and enjoy them. With practice, you can learn to ride the waves of feeling without being upset or needing to suppress any of your emotions.

With practice you can learn to ride the waves of feeling without being upset or needing to suppress them.

Regular use of the HEART Techniques will help you solve the mystery of love.

I'm not saying that it will always be easy — there will be times when tension and conflicts still come up in your relationships. But now you have the formula to help you resolve all of those uncomfortable emotions and get back down to the love.

I hope you make good use of all of the techniques offered in this book. Remember — they don't work if you don't use them. The time and energy you invest in working with the HEART Techniques will pay off in the increased harmony, peace and joy you will experience in all of your relationships!

Your ability to love is the most precious gift you have. Don't waste it. Use every moment of your life as an opportunity to give and receive love. Soon you'll notice that life has ceased to be a struggle. When your heart is filled with love, life becomes a vacation.

Love can work if you know how to make it work, and now you do. Share your new knowledge and this book with the people you care about. Dedicate yourself to making love work in your life and in the world, and the rewards for yourself and those you love will be priceless.

When you heart is filled with love, life is like a big vacation.

DR. JOHN GRAY

Cordially Invites You...
to enrich your relationships
through audio cassette recordings of his seminars.

1. The *Relationship* **Series** provides a new, exciting and inspirational approach to enriching relationships through understanding the complementary differences between men and women. In six sessions, Dr. Gray explores how to:

(1) Enrich Relationships,
(2) Increase Intimacy,
(3) Transform Sex into Making Love,
(4) Understand Men,
(5) Understand Women, and
(6) Improve Communication.

Each session consists of two audio cassettes recorded live from one of Dr. Gray's seminars. The complete Relationship Series consists of 12 audio cassettes.

2. The *Healing the Heart* **Series** provides an innovative step by step approach to heal the heart from the painful influences of your past and to create loving and positive attitudes. In six sessions, Dr. Gray explores how to:

(1) Create Great Success,
(2) Overcome Fear and Anxiety,
(3) Increase Self-acceptance and Self-esteem,
(4) Heal the Emotional Wounds of Childhood,
(5) Release Resentments through Forgiveness, and
(6) Understand the Ten Stages of Spiritual Growth.

Each session consists of two audio cassettes recorded live from one of Dr. Gray's seminars. Each of the first five sessions contains a presentation, a question and answer session and a healing process designed to be used again and again.

The five healing processes are: *The Success Process, The Overcoming Fear Process, The Self-acceptance Process, The Re-parenting Process* and *The Forgiveness Process*. The complete Healing Series consists of 12 audio cassettes.

3. The *What You Feel, You Can Heal* **Series** expands upon the basic information contained in the book. Dr. Gray inspires you to love and accept yourself more each day through sharing stories and examples from his personal life. The complete series consists of six audio cassettes.

The *Relationship* Series	$99.70 (12 cassettes)
The *Healing the Heart* Series	$99.70 (12 cassettes)
The *What You Feel, You Can Heal* Series	$59.95 (6 cassettes)

You may order any or all of the tape series by sending a check or money order to: Heart Publishing, 20 Sunnyside Ave., Suite A-130, Mill Valley, CA 94941. Use Mastercard or Visa by calling (415) 381-5735. Add 10% for shipping (plus 6% for California orders).